# GLOBAL

# MELTDOWN

A Story of the End Time

By

Tim Doyle

World rights reserved. This book or any portion thereof may not be copied or reproduced in any form or manner whatever, except as provided by law, without the written permission of the publisher, except by a reviewer who may quote brief passages in a review.

This book is sold with the understanding that the publisher is not engaged in giving spiritual, legal, medical, or other professional advice. If authoritative advice is needed, the reader should seek the counsel of a competent professional

---

Copyright © 2012 Tim Doyle
ISBN-13: 978-1-57258-909-4 (Paperback)
Library of Congress Control Number: 2011908334

Edited by Jon Usher, Alayne Floyd, Sharon Clark and Brenda Doyle.
Cover design by Jaclyn Burford, David Johns.
Cover photographs taken by:
Robert A Eplett, Richard White, Andrea Booher, Patsy Lynch,
Larry Lerner, Liz Roll, Leif Skoogfors, Michael Mancino,
Casey Deschong, Earl Armstrong, Leo 'Jace' Anderson,
Courtesy of Fema News Photo. Used by permission.

Book title font created by Aenigma Fonts.
Author's name font for cover by Fonthead Design.

The events and stories in this end time story are strictly fictional.

Scripture quotations are taken from the Holy Bible, New International Version, NIV Copyright 1973, 1978, 1984, by International Bible Society. Used by permission of Zondervan Publishing House. All rights reserved.

To obtain discounts for larger quantities of this book or to schedule a Prophecy Seminar email: doyle.noteinvestor@gmail.com

# Readers are excited about *Global Meltdown*

*"Tim has captured end–time truths as they are presented in the Bible and prophetic writings. And through narrative has given us an exciting book to prepare us for last-day events."*
Pastor Ron Ray
Hot Springs, Arkansas

*"I was in on the writing of the 'Global Meltdown' from the very beginning and therefore feel I have a special investment in it. It is well written, fast moving, and will hold your attention to the end. It is written in an exciting story form, while at the same time conveying in an easy to understand format some pertinent, vital Bible truths that will help prepare you for the coming tribulation time. It climaxes with the Second

*Coming of Jesus, which the Apostle Paul calls "the blessed hope" of the Church.*

*While the characters and the story itself are purely fictitious, the struggles, hardships, sorrows, and joys portrayed, may well parallel the actual happenings of God's faithful during the time of trouble. The key end time events portrayed are actually based on the prophecies of the Bible, and thus have the potential of enabling the reader to be informed as to what is soon coming upon the earth.*

*You may find yourself identifying with some of the characters by rejoicing with them in their times of happiness, and crying with them in their sorrows.*

*Their inner joy and peace, while suffering bitter persecution, will most certainly inspire you to covet their experience with the Lord.*

*It is my prayer that you will discover this book to be both pleasurable reading and life changing as well."*

**Carroll Graybeal**

Lay Pastor and Guest Columnist for the Malvern Daily Record

Tim wrote a great book. It instantly caught my attention and had it all the way through the book and I learned quite a bit too. There was not a boring moment. It was packed full of adventure, fear, teaching, and prophecy. I have heard many stories about the end of time, but this really summed it up. I also believe that this is going to happen; how the Sunday law was passed, the persecution, Gods hand over His followers, and of course the second coming. This is all true and has been for all humanity. Read this book and understand what choice we have to make. I hope you make the right choice. I'll see you in heaven. Thanks again for this book of the "Global Meltdown!"

Dakota Ray- 15 year old student now, at Ozark academy, Gentry Arkansas


"This is definitely a book for the end of time."

A. Jan Marcussen

Pastor, Evangelist and author of 'the National Sunday Law book'

(Downloaded free @ reg6)

"Tim has created a whirlwind scenario of his new book **Global Meltdown** which will keep you spellbound right to the very last page!

Woven into this carefully and tightly-knit plot are the Bible Truths that we as Christians must know if we are to be ready for Jesus when He triumphantly returns to take His true followers to their Heavenly home. Tim has handled very well the 'tough' questions that Christians and non Christians alike are asking about God, Jesus, and moral, ethical and spiritual issues. This book is a must-read for everyone- you don't want to miss even one chapter!"

David Sloan, Dr of Natural and Homeopathic Medicine.

# Acknowledgments

I would like to thank all those who shared their thoughts and honest opinions about this book. Among these are Carroll and Judy Graybeal who have been true friends. Then there's Marie Judd (who is like a real sister and friend) and the Eaglebear family who listened to me as I read the manuscript and refused to take a break until it was all read. Their excitement really encouraged me. Also Michael Wolford, my Pastor and mentor encouraged me and kept me motivated. Then there is Eugene Prewitt, former bible teacher at Ouachita Hills College in Amity, Arkansas, (At this writing, He and his wife Heidi are ministering with Amazing Facts). Eugene assured me that the manuscript was theologically sound.

Special thanks go to my wife Brenda of 19 years, who patiently bore with me and put much work into helping make this book a reality. I have grown to appreciate and value her more and more as the years go by. Also many thanks go to my friend, Sharon Clark, who is a well-published author and teacher (just two of her many talents). She coached me greatly along the way. If it weren't for her and the valuable information she provided, this manuscript wouldn't be where it is today. Thanks so very much!...Then there's my daughter Jaclyn Burford who designed my cover, arranged the pictures for me and came up with the awesome font for Global Meltdown. She has a natural talent. Thanks so much, sweetie! We don't want to forget my brother in Christ, David Johns from Present Solutions, who has worked with Jaclyn to complete the cover design with their up-to-date software and expertise. They have been a real blessing. Then there's my dear spiritual brother and friend Jon Usher who is multi-talented, along with being a wonderful teacher. With unceasing labor he edited my manuscript. Words cannot express the gratitude I feel for all you have done. You were God sent Jon. Also we have Alayne Floyd who helped with last minute editing that was necessary to complete manuscript before publishing. Thanks so much!

And most of all I would like to thank my Heavenly Father for inspiring me to write this book in the first place and using so many of His faithful children to encourage me all along the way.

# Prologue

"*Foss News! Where you get unbiased news—with Jake Bellow.*"

"*Today's top story: 'Gooble Facing Bankruptcy unless Economic Changes Soon Take Place'. Gooble, one of the world's largest internet services, is tottering on the brink of bankruptcy. Negotiations are underway with the U. S. government for a bailout and takeover which could save thousands of jobs worldwide. The government bailout package for the floundering corporation will probably top two hundred billion dollars! At this time when our country is already in debt for well over eighteen trillion dollars, economic experts are warning that if things don't turn around for Gooble, it could be the final straw that breaks the back of the global economy.*"

"*For more on this story and other related news, let's go to Pat Harvey, live in Washington D.C. Are you there, Pat?*"

"*I'm here, Jake.*"

"*Tell us what's going on in Washington?*"

"*Jake, there is a large crowd gathered outside the White House. Some of the protestors are carrying signs criticizing the government's handling of the national economic crisis. Others say something about saving the family. I have seen hundreds of 'Ban Abortion' t-shirts. There's a huge sign just behind us that says 'Sunday Is the Day of Worship!' There's a band playing somewhere close by and a lot of excitement...What?...Oh, Okay...Thank you!...I'm being told that the Secretary of State has finished his briefing, and now the President is going to take questions.*"

"*Mr. President,*" a reporter asked, "*in the midst of our nation's current economic downslide, particularly in the housing industry, with historical numbers of foreclosures not only in Arkansas, California, Florida, and Idaho, but now spreading to the rest of the country—a condition that has surpassed the Great Depression and is growing worse all the time—and with the environmental disasters that have been crippling industry and agriculture for the last few years here in the U. S., do you have some practical solutions to these crises that threaten our national security?*"

"My good people of America and around the world, I believe with all my heart that as bad as it is for many of you just now, times will soon change and we will come out stronger than we have ever been. Corporate greed has brought our country down to where it is today, but I want you to know that this is going to change. CEOs of all businesses here in America are now responsible—and answerable—to the government for all their financial decisions. All bonuses, pay raises, and salary caps have to be approved by the U.S. Government. We are going to put a stop to corporate greed and tax evaders once and for all!"

"Mr. President, is there an immediate answer to the hundreds of thousands of families that have lost their homes and jobs and are living on the streets of America?"

"Ummm, well, we are now working on a solution in conjunction with state and local governments and church leaders. We will be making an announcement soon. We want the American people to know that the decisions that we make are for the best interest of society and the world."

"What are these changes and—"

"That's all I can tell you for now."

"Jake, as the President is leaving the pressroom (We are told for Los Angeles and yet another disaster briefing), new questions come to mind: What changes is the President talking about? Why is the government calling on churches to help make changes? And how will this be for the best interest of society and the world? At this point, there seems to be more questions than answers. For Foss News in Washington, I'm Pat Harvey."

"And I'm Jake Bellow in our New York studios. Stay with Foss for all the latest developments!"

# Chapter 1

"Come, Girls, we have to go or we'll be late for Church."

"We're coming, Dad!"

"How are you feeling today, Lisa? Is your fibromyalgia acting up again? I heard you tossing and turning and moaning most of the night."

"Oh, I should be okay, John. I didn't sleep much though. I finally resorted to taking painkillers again. After that I didn't do too badly."

"I'm sorry that you have to suffer like you do—and that you can't work anymore. I know you miss that. I wish I could do more to help."

"It's okay, John. God knows best."

"Shannon, make sure Kimmy brings her Bible for her primary class; they're having a sword drill today."

"Okay, Mom!"

"Mommy, since I'm almost nine years old, does Shannon have to keep taking care of me? I'm a big girl now."

"Well, Kimmy, talk to me in a couple months when you turn nine; then perhaps we can make some changes. Okay?"

"Okay, Mom."

"It's hard to believe you are going on nine already and that Shannon is twelve now. Where does the time go?"

"Let's roll!" said Dad.

"Can you bring the cooler for me, John. The food's in it already. And could you grab my Bible. Put it in a WallyWorld bag—it's so wet out there! This weather does me in. I'm in too much pain right now to carry it and me."

"Sure, Honey."

"Where are all those emergency vehicles going?" Kimmy asked her Dad as they were driving to church.

"I'm not sure! But with all the rain we've been having, there's been talk that the dam is getting full and hard to contain. They can only release so much water before there's a possibility of a flood. I've heard that homes in Hot Springs and the surrounding areas could be affected."

After arriving at the church, John said to Lisa, "Look! There's Bob and his daughter Michelle. They're finally back from their three year mission trip to Africa. His wife's death must have been so hard… I'm going to go talk with him. Maybe I can be some comfort."

"Dad, can I visit with Michelle?"

"Sure, but don't be late for your class."

"Okay, Dad."

"Bob, it's great seeing you. Give me a hug, Brother. We've all missed you tremendously. I'm very sorry about Debbie."

"Thanks, John. After she got the cholera, she only lasted a few days. We tried everything to save her, but nothing worked." After they conversed for some time, Bob's expression changed and with tears in his eyes he said, "John, please pray for Michelle."

"Why, what's the matter? Did she catch a disease, too?"

"No, it's not that. It's just that she's been getting very rebellious. Ever since Debbie died, she blames God and wants nothing to do with Him. I even caught her drinking and smoking. I don't understand, John. Why is she turning her back on God?"

"I'm so sorry, Bob! I'll ask my wife to put her on our prayer list. You might not have heard that Lisa was diagnosed recently with fibromyalgia. I can't totally relate to what you're going through with your loss—or even with Michelle—but I can relate to some of the problems of dealing with a debilitating disease."

Meanwhile Michelle called Shannon around to the side of the church. Shannon tried to comfort Michelle, "I'm sorry about your Mother, it must be hard on you and your Dad."

"Yeah, I guess" said Michelle, trying to hold back the tears, and then abruptly, "Hey! I want you to try something," as she pulled some cigarettes from her purse. "They're really cool. Nothing like the ones made here."

As she went to light up the cigarette, Shannon exclaimed, "Wait, what are you doing? I don't do that!"

"Come on, you're a big girl now."

"It's just that—."

"What!? You're not chicken are you?"

"Jesus doesn't—."

"Oh stop with that religious talk. Do you want to try it or not?"

"No, thanks!"

"Well, then, you're no friend of mine!" Michelle blurted out.

"Wait, please!" Shannon pleaded.

"No, don't talk to me, you geek!"

Just then Shannon's mom came outside, "Come in Shannon, your class is starting."

During the class, as Shannon glanced back, Michelle was whispering something to a boy, and they both laughed. After class Michelle made a snide remark before entering the Sanctuary. "Ah, there's Mama's girl. Better hurry, you don't want to get Mama worried again."

During the service the pastor began his sermon in an unusual way, with a concerned tone of voice. "Last night I woke at 2:30 a.m. with a heavy heart. The Lord impressed me to give a different message than what I originally planned. I have been awake all night studying end time events, and I feel strongly impressed to share with you the nearness of Christ's return—in a way that I have never done before in my ministry. Times as we know them are about to drastically change. Look around at your brothers and sisters. It could be that some of us will not see—" The Pastor cleared his throat and still had a hard time getting the words out, "—another Sabbath!"

"What's the pastor saying?" Shannon whispered to her Mom.

"I'm not sure. Just listen."

Meanwhile, in the back Michelle whispered to another friend, "Oh, give it a break. Is he going to start begging for money now?"

"I don't want to sound like an 'alarmist' or scare you. My message will be short today."

"Amen!" whispered Michelle.

"If you have not yet been serious about your walk with God, please surrender your heart to Him now. We are living in difficult times. Some of you have taken in other families after they lost their jobs and homes. And God sees and recognizes your sacrifices and your love. I believe we are living in the time just before Jesus returns. The Constitution has been conveniently—." As the pastor was speaking sirens were heard, growing louder until doors banged open, and the local Sheriff and emergency personnel came rushing through the church doors. "What is this?" exclaimed the pastor.

"We're sorry to interrupt your church service, Reverend, but we have an emergency situation, and we have to evacuate everyone. Blakely Dam is filling up fast and about to breach. Everyone must leave the area as quickly and safely as they can. You will be notified when you can go back to your homes."

Crying, screaming, and general bedlam erupted as many of the churchgoers were panic-stricken. A few members remained calm and tried to keep order. Seconds later vehicles were flying down the church driveway and adding to the mass chaos that was developing all over Hot Springs and surrounding areas. Accidents, ensuing traffic jams, and people of all ages running for their lives swirled around John and his family as they tried to drive to higher ground. Lisa had tuned to the local emergency radio station.

"Citizens of Hot Springs and surrounding areas, we are asking that you please follow evacuation routes out of the flood plain as directed by emergency personnel. All military, fire, emergency medical service providers, FEMA workers, and volunteers, please report to your local hospital, clinic, or nursing home. You are being asked to assist with the evacuation and the directing of traffic."

"Mommy, Daddy, I'm scared; what's going to happen? Where will we go?"

"I'm not sure yet, Kimmy. God has a plan."

Smash!

"Dad, Mom, did you see that. A car just crashed into that delivery vehicle over there? Now a man has jumped out and is beating up the driver who hit him."

"Daddy, Daddy, please stop him!"

"It's okay, Kimmy. Those two tall men are calming him down. I wonder where they came from; I didn't notice them at first."

"John, why don't we pray?"

"That's a good idea, Lisa. Would you pray?"

"Dear Heavenly Father, please help that man and all the angry and scared people. And please," she hoarsely whispered, "please, draw near to us. We need you to help us."

"It's OK, Honey. Hang in there."

Through her sobs, Lisa continued, "God please protect us and keep everyone safe while we try to get out of the area. We claim Psalm 91, 'He who dwells in the shelter of the Most High will rest in the shadow of the Almighty. I will say of the Lord, He is my refuge and my fortress, my God, in whom I trust. . . . under His wings you will find refuge. . . . A thousand may fall at your side, ten thousand at your right hand, but it will not come near you"[1] Thank you, Jesus! Amen."

"Thanks, Lisa. Girls, I want to tell you something. This may be the only chance I have to share what's on my heart. I know I've been too busy with work and church activities, and I haven't been consistent with family worship, nor have I spent much quality time with you. I'm sorry. I see now that I've neglected my most important duty, which is preparing you for eternity and the difficult times we are experiencing. I really haven't paid much attention until the pastor started speaking this morning. Not until then did I realize my spiritual condition. I know you have seen me in church teaching, preaching, and performing my duties as an elder, but deep down inside my walk with God has been empty."

"Honey, watch that driver!"

"Thanks, Lisa. I see him. Also I haven't been sharing my faith with others like I should have been. I thought that if I could just make my family happy, provide a nice home and nice things and give you a Christian education, then all would be fine. I know there's nothing wrong with having these things, but when they come first before our duty to God and others, then we lose our relationship—our saving closeness—with God and each other. Your Mother tried to help me see that, but I was blinded to it until this morning. Can you forgive—"

The radio announcer interrupted, *"We have an urgent message for all residents of Hot Springs and surrounding areas: Blakely Dam has just burst. We urge you to go to a higher elevation immediately!"*

"Dad, there's a bad accident ahead!"

"That was close! It's getting really rough out there."

"Where are we going to go?"

"I'm not sure, Shannon."

As they tried to push their way forward, a loudspeaker from a helicopter above them echoed the same evacuation message and disappeared into the dark clouds from which a steady rain continued to fall.

"Daddy, how can we get out with all these cars around? Everyone is leaving their cars and running."

Suddenly Lisa yelled out, "Dear God, help us please!"

As chaos escalated all around them, John told the children to stay seated and make sure their full seat belts were fastened. "I'm putting the truck in four-wheel drive. We're going off the road."

"Honey, we'll never make it."

"Pray for us, Lisa, we're going!"

"No, John, please!"

"Hang on!"

As the girls started screaming and crying, John apologized for yelling. "I love you all! Just hang on!"

"This is Jake Bellow coming to you live on Foss News! with a fast-breaking story from Hot Springs, Arkansas. Jim Bell, who flew in to Hot Springs this morning after hearing how floodings were taking place in Arkansas, is reporting from a helicopter flying above the area where, just minutes ago, Blakely Dam burst, sending millions of gallons of water raging through this well-known Southern community on a very busy Saturday morning. Here's Jim to give us an update on what's happening there."

"Early this morning at around 9:00," Jim began, "emergency personnel responded to an alarm from a security system in Mountain Pine, Arkansas, where Blakely Dam is located. This Dam sits above the entire region; it separates Lake Ouachita from Lake Hamilton and Lake Catherine. These lakes in this popular tourist region, surround the Hot Springs area. At approximately 1:00 pm central time the dam burst due to the excessive rains. Residents in this area are being evacuated. The majority of the lower plains are being inundated, where most of the population is centered, and the waters continue to rise;"

"Jim," Jake interrupted, "what is being done for these residents?"

"Live footage is now being shown as rescue teams are reaching survivors on high slopes and securing them. Some—wait a minute, it looks as though a few survivors have made it to the top of the ridges in what appears to be four-wheel drive vehicles—I even see some horses and other animals. We are unable to get a close-up at this time, but you can see the rushing waters—trees, all kinds of debris and entire houses swept away just below them. I've never seen such devastation. It's hard to tell whether any will escape. God help them."

"Amen."

# Chapter 2

"*And now we go to Pat Harvey reporting to you from just outside the White House in Washington, D.C.*"

"Government leaders are meeting with the United Nations and worldwide church representatives to discuss solutions for the deepening woes of America and the rest of the world. The President is asking for churches to unite in this great crisis and for every person to set aside Sunday as a time for worship, family time, and prayer. Here is the President now."

"My fellow Americans, due to increasing difficulties that we have been experiencing in our nation: the economy sagging, banks closing, automobile industries going bankrupt, floods, fires, earthquakes, hurricanes, tornadoes, famines, and other natural disasters, I am asking that we as a nation seek God's guidance. Not only in our nation but around the world these issues are of great concern. With all of these things happening on a global scale, I am afraid that we have somehow displeased God very much. Therefore, I am asking that we, the citizens of the global community, would set aside each Sunday to reunite with our families."

The President's statement was met with thunderous applause.

"We have become greedy. We have kicked God out of our schools and the workplace and even out of our nations. Families are disintegrating and divorce rates are out of control. And no wonder! Families have no time together anymore because both parents are working. I believe—and our great Christian leaders concur—that our nation is experiencing these troubles because we have forgotten God. Our country began well as a Christian nation, but over time, especially as technology has developed, we have become a materialistic society. We need to get back to the sacredness of true worship and the family. Therefore, as President of the United States of America, and because we are a Christian nation, I am signing into law Sunday legislation that will enforce those changes that will once more bring us into the favor of Almighty God."

Again loud and sustained applause interrupted the President's speech.

*"This legislation will allow families time for each other. Businesses will, of course, be closed on Sunday, so that we can all spend this day with our families. Essential businesses that cannot be safely or practically closed weekly will only be allowed to work their employees half a day every other Sunday. Perhaps as a result of this national decree, God will once again smile upon us."*

A standing ovation delayed the President's departure for nearly half an hour.

Meanwhile during the President's address chaos reigned in Hot Springs. "Daddy!!" Kimmy yelled out, "We're stuck and the water is almost caught up to our truck!"

"I know. Lisa, I need your help. Can you drive while I push us out?"

"Okay, John!"

"Let the truck rock back and forth. When I give the go ahead, hit the gas—hard!" As John pushed and Lisa worked the gas pedal, the tires spun deeper ruts in the front and back.

"John, we've got to get out of here—and we don't have much time."

"Yes, I know, Honey." As the swirling winds began to increase in intensity, John yelled, "Shannon, stay with Kimmy and go to higher ground. We'll meet you up there!"

"But—I'm scared…"

"It will be okay! Go!!" As the girls ran up the hill, a sound could be heard like that of an approaching freight train.

"John, John, look out!"

# Chapter 3

"Foss News! Coming back to you again live with Jim Bell from Hot Springs, Arkansas. Jim, what's happening there?"

"Jake, landslides are occurring throughout the region due to the torrential downpours. And now the area has been hit with horizontal winds with velocities reaching sixty miles an hour. Buildings, trees, towers, and vehicles are sliding into the rising waters. Rescue teams are working frantically to save any survivors. Just now I'm seeing a team working to save two girls on a slope before the landslides reach them. With slumping ground all around them and these tornado-like conditions, it is uncertain whether they will succeed."

"Thanks, Jim. Keep us posted. We return now to Ted Ritsema who is keeping us updated on conditions in Los Angeles after last Thursday's catastrophic earthquake. Ted, are you there?"

"Yes, thanks, Jake. Rescuers are finding few new survivors in Los Angeles and surrounding Southern California communities in the aftermath of the 9.8 earthquake that devastated this heavily populated area two days ago, perhaps the greatest disaster of the century. Portions of the coastal landmass, including entire communities, continue sloughing off into the ocean with little or no warning. The number of lives lost is astronomical; property damage, beyond estimation. There are not enough rescue units left to begin to handle all the needs. After flying over the region today, the President has declared the West Coast a Disaster Area and under a State of Emergency, which, of course, also imposes martial law."

"Ted, don't you mean the Los Angeles area—Southern California—is under a State of Emergency?"

"Because of all the disasters in L.A., Jake, people are rioting all over the West Coast. So a State of Emergency has been issued for the entire West Coast. In all the years that I have been a reporter, I have never seen anything like this. I have never witnessed this kind of... as Ted is choking up trying to regain his composure he manages to get it out, abject terror—total panic—that I have seen these last 48 hours.

*Everywhere I hear people expressing their fear that the end of the world is here. Local authorities cannot control the riots and looting that are taking place. Hopefully more outside help will be able to come soon."*

"Thanks, Ted."

"You bet, Jake!"

"So, now we have California, Arkansas, Florida, and Idaho under a State of Emergency. The death toll in these states is in the hundreds of thousands with the numbers continually rising. Perhaps God is trying to speak to our nation. The latest hurricane in Florida, the worst ever in recorded history for that area, has affected the entire Gulf Coast. Damage is in the multiple billions of dollars. Tourism and the real estate market have collapsed. The United Nations, already loaded down with disasters around the world, has resolved to send aid—eventually. Everywhere insurance companies are going bankrupt, and homeowners are being forced to pay for their own losses. Coming up in the next hour, FEMA and other emergency support group leaders will be joining us live right here on Foss News! with instructions on how to best handle these disasters."

"But first back to Hot Springs, Arkansas, and Jim Bell. Jim, what developments have taken place since we last talked?"

"It appears that the waters have stopped rising in the area. Interstate 30 is closed for several miles, choking the main artery of North/South commerce and transportation. As the water levels rose, they extended past Interstate 30, even reaching as far as Malvern, several miles from the Interstate. Other small communities, including Diamondhead, are presently under water. All these areas are still being evacuated, leaving other roads and highways slow going at best. Amazingly, however, in the city of Hot Springs there are a few spots—surprisingly in the lower levels—that were virtually untouched."

"Jim, how is that possible?"

"It's nothing short of a miracle. Rescuers are landing now in the parking lot of one of these locations. Several survivors have taken refuge at a church off of highway 270 bypass. The sign on the hill identifies it as the, the—Jake, I can't quite make out the sign because of the high winds and this incessant rain—oh, well, there went the sign! Anyway, all the buildings on top of the hill have remained untouched. According to survivors, worship services were being held at the church when they were interrupted by the Sheriff's Department asking the members to evacuate the area. Few were able to actually leave though because the only road that led out of the church—Weston Road, I think—was jammed with abandoned vehicles, leaving almost everyone trapped. And just a short distance away, Lake Hamilton was out of control."

"So where did local residents go, Jim?"

"Many in the immediate area who couldn't escape ran up to the highest elevation where the church stands. No logical explanation can be found as to why this hill (which isn't very high!) was not flooded. Rescue teams are taking no chances, and these residents are being flown to a safer area. According to eyewitnesses, some families left the church shortly before the dam broke. We have with us now the pastor of the church. He was flown to this temporary emergency base camp and has been ministering to other survivors."

"Pastor Sven, could we talk with you? What are your thoughts right now as you see the destruction that has been going on all around you?"

"I must say, I have mixed feelings."

"What do you mean?"

"Well, I am saddened because of the great loss of lives. On the other hand, I am grateful that God has spared the majority of our church family and many members of our community. If this tragedy had occurred on any day other than the Sabbath, many more of my members would have died. I am not at all surprised, however, at the events taking place here—and in other states."

"Why do you say that?"

"Well, the Bible does foretell that cataclysmic events will occur and intensify just before Jesus' second coming."

"So are you saying God is punishing our nation or something?"

"We as a country were known for our belief in God. In its beginning our nation stood on Christian principles."

"So are you saying that we are a Christian nation? Do you believe this would give our government the right to legislate religious laws?"

"On the contrary, we are a nation that was *founded* on Christian principles, but we are *not* a Christian nation."

"So what's the difference?"

"To quote a great religious leader: 'Christianity is not a culture-creating thing, but rather a culture-influencing one.' Shall I define more specifically what I mean?"

"It might help…"

"Take the New Testament Scriptures, for example. Throughout the New Testament it is implied that the state is a secular institution, established by God Himself to regulate, as best it can with the insights available to it and with the resources at its command, the things of this age or era. In the New Testament vision, the State, being itself a creature of God's common grace, walks with the resources which that non-redemptive grace makes available."[1]

"Uh, could you explain what that means in simple terms, Pastor."

"In other words, the State has nothing to do with enforcing any particular religious dogma, or set of beliefs; but rather it is there to enforce civil laws that are unrelated to any particular religion. Once they overstep their God-given authority, they violate the religious freedom that even God Himself does not violate. Like Nebuchadnezzar, King of Babylon. He tried at first to enforce a decree that everyone bow down to his image of gold. Then later, after seeing how God saved three men from his fiery furnace, he threatened that anyone who refused to worship the true God would be punished.[2] In both instances, he was wrong, regardless of his intentions. The state should never attempt to force citizens to submit to its ideas of God's requirements, no matter what the circumstances might be. God never forces us to serve Him. When the civil government enacts religious laws persecution will inevitably result."

"Okay, Pastor, what do *you* call these calamities taking place in our nation and around the world then?"

"If a man—or a government—chooses to follow a course in violation of God's moral principles, it's like ignoring road signs: ultimately, he is going to suffer the consequences. If one chooses to challenge the law of gravity and jumps off the top of a building into the street below, he is going to suffer the consequences: serious injury or even death, regardless of his motives or intentions. In the same way, if men violate the law of God, they will have to suffer the consequences.

'Sew to the wind; reap the whirlwind'. As I see it, this earth is experiencing global cooling."

"What do you mean?"

"In Matthew 24:12 Jesus says, 'Because of the increase of wickedness, the love of most will grow cold;' So you see we have a moral dilemma: a global cooling of men's hearts. The heart is where the greatest change needs to take place, not in civil enactments and penalties to force everyone to obey God. Heart changing is God's business. By the way, Jesus tells us another way that we can know His coming is at hand. In Matthew 24:5 He says, 'Many will come in my name, claiming, I am the Christ, and will deceive many. I'm sure you've heard of Jim Jones, David Koresh, and other imposters. Then we have—"

"Ah, excuse me, Pastor. We have to take a break. Back to you, Jake."

# Chapter 4

"Connie Dunn, who is covering the Washington State story on same sex couples and recent laws in their favor has an important update on recent events. Connie, give us an update."

"Sure Jake. Only days after Washington state lawmakers passed the 'Hate Crime Bill' (A bill that is the pattern for pending federal legislation) making it illegal for churches to speak against the 'same sex' partner lifestyle, homosexual activists from all over the U.S. and even from Canada have taken full advantage of the new law to protest against what they are calling illegal discrimination by certain church groups in the Seattle/Tacoma area. They are lining up in front of churches that are non-compliant and denying their members entrance, even swinging baseball bats and throwing rocks at the defenseless members and knocking them to the ground."

"Wait a minute, Connie. Where are the police?"

"The police are just standing by and watching these people almost beaten to death. We attempted to get live coverage, but activist groups are not allowing reporters to come within range. If any attempt is made, they start throwing rocks and other objects at us and our cameras. We had to resort to coverage by phone conversations."

"Thanks, Connie. Don't take any chances!"

"Right!"

"And now an update from Charlie Adams, who's bringing us live coverage from Boise, Idaho. Charlie, are we connected?"

"Yes...but I can barely hear you over the winds!"

"Charlie, tell us what's happening there?"

"Sure, Jake! As wildfires rage across the Idaho panhandle, fire fighters and helicopter teams work frantically to bring them under control. With the heavy winds, however, it is nearly impossible to slow the fires down. Residents of Northern Idaho have been asked to evacuate. There's no telling how far these fires will go; certainly as long as heavy winds continue there is no end in sight. The state of Idaho has been declared a disaster area and FEMA is enforcing the evacuation order."

*"Thanks, Charlie!"*

Meanwhile survivors were fighting for their lives in Hot Springs. When Shannon and Kimmy were rescued, Shannon pleaded with her rescuers, "My mother and father! Please help them! They're still down below."

"Attention! All emergency personnel," the helicopter pilot yelled out over the loud speaker. "Keep your eyes open for a man and woman in their late thirties or so. Two girls who have been rescued say that their parents were just below us trying to push their truck out of the mud where the landslide occurred."

After some time, however, reports of a massive landslide that had swept everything on the hillside into the waters below gave little hope of any survivors.

"Returning again to Jim Bell as he brings us live coverage from Hot Springs. Jim, can you catch us up on the developments there"

"Sure, Jake! Rescue attempts are still in progress. While a few survivors have made it to safety, recent massive landslides have left little hope for many still missing. Some, however, were fortunate indeed. I've been talking to Pastor Sven of a Hot Springs Church whose buildings and members were miraculously protected while almost the entire city is under water."

"Pastor Sven," Jim began "before we continue our discussion where we left off, can you explain why the flood waters never reached the top of the hill where your church is located?"

"Prayer." the pastor calmly responded.

"Excuse me? Did you say prayer?"

"Yes, I did!"

"Please explain."

"When we realized there was nowhere to escape, all the church members that were left and the area residents who had run up the hill prayed to God for protection."

"Are you saying that your church members prayed with members of other denominations?"

"We surely did!"

"That's good! It is truly remarkable, Pastor, how your church buildings, remaining members, and local residents who fled here survived the flood. I understand from some of your members that your church had planned to hold some meetings for the public."

"Yes. That is true. We still plan to hold them, whether in Hot Springs or elsewhere. Meetings like these are the focus of our world church ministry. Our church members conduct them in locations all over the U.S. and around the world."

"You said the members. Did you mean they assist while the pastors conduct the meetings?"

"No, to the contrary, the lay people, mostly consisting of the younger generation, actually conduct the meetings, while we pastors oversee the work and offer our assistance when needed."

"This is very unusual indeed! What will be discussed at these meetings?"

"There will be several topics taken from the Bible. They concentrate on the signs of the times, how to avoid the 'mark of the beast', and how to be prepared to meet Jesus when He returns."

"Thank you for taking time out to talk with us today. I'll be looking forward to attending those meetings. What are *your* future plans?"

"I'm not sure yet—my first responsibility is to my family and my church family, of course—but knowing our members as I do, I believe, as has happened in many disaster areas, that they will help out in any way they can. It seems that disasters are becoming almost common place. But God's people are always there, forgetting about their own comforts and assisting others in any way they can. Not only in church organized relief efforts for distributing blankets and water and survival packets, but also lay people everywhere are answering the call to help, even if it means personal sacrifice. It's great to be a part of that!"

"We have been speaking with Pastor Sven, live from Hot Springs, Arkansas."

# Chapter 5

"And now World News! with Dan Boyle."

"Thank you, Jake. Tomorrow the President and major world leaders are having a summit meeting to discuss international economic and moral issues and the possibility of joining hands with faith-based organizations to solve the escalating world crises. There are church groups that have expressed concern over their communions participating directly in the solution of these issues. They believe that it is a uniting of church and state and are concerned that religious liberties will ultimately be affected. Some go as far as to say that if church and state clasp hands, then the religious liberties that our founding fathers worked so hard to protect will be weakened or lost all together. Ultimately they're concerned that the civil government will enact laws that violate the conscience and one's moral obligation to God."

"Dan, how is that possible? The Constitution protects religious freedom."

"When the state steps in, they say, and enacts religious laws, they are in effect standing in the place of God. The President is assuring the American people that such laws would only help society get back on its feet. They will not be for discriminating against one's religious backgrounds or beliefs. Some argue that the Sunday law that was just passed violates certain religious denominations' beliefs already. They say that no matter how good a law may seem to be, if it is religious in nature, it will ultimately lead to discrimination. Others are enraged that these critics are not working toward the common good by uniting in prayer and family time on Sundays, but are instead causing disunity and disruption."

"Okay, Dan! Appreciate the update. I understand too that you're following events in New York with Gooble. What's happening there?

"Decisions are being made as we speak, Jake. There are many concerned citizens that are protesting these decisions. Gooble is definitely accepting a bail out from the government and is giving control over to them. Now, say many, the feds can control the internet any way they choose. There has been discussion on silencing those who make political statements that the government disagrees with. What is also causing concern is a rumor that the government has already been using Facelook to gather information by using their over sixteen hundred employees. If they gain full control, personal emails will be able to be accessed and who knows where that may lead."

"Thanks, Dan! Now back to Hot Springs and Jim Bell."

"Survivors are still being found in the Hot Springs area, Jake. Video footage has just come in that shows a rescuer saving people clinging to a tower that crashed onto one of the slopes where landslides occurred. This tower is stuck between two ridges some distance away from where it originally fell. Flood waters are still rising. Report has come in that rescuers were able to save three people from the tower area. So far several thousand have been rescued from the massive dam burst in Mountain Pine, Arkansas. Rescuers are hopeful there may still be more survivors from this devastating disaster."

"We hope so, too, Jim!"

"Now going back to Idaho with Charlie Adams. You say you have good news from Idaho, Charles."

"Yes, I do, Jake! Clouds from out of nowhere have come in, and rain is pouring down, putting out the fires that seemed just hours ago to be uncontrollable. It is being said by church leaders that God is smiling down on His people in Idaho now that the Sunday laws are here and families will be able to spend more time together on the Lord's Day. It's their prayer that other states will take this law seriously and follow suit. Some states in the Bible Belt that already have Sunday blue laws are getting serious about enforcing them."

"How are they enforcing these laws?"

"To start with they are going to impose a five hundred dollar fine on any business that tries to open their doors on Sunday. There is also discussion about imposing a one hundred dollar fine to individuals in these states if they are caught working outside even on their own property. Other nations are closely following the progress of these laws; some are imposing even more severe penalties for violations. Provinces in Canada and England have in the past enforced Sunday laws with much more severe penalties. At one point chain grocery stores in Ontario, Canada that we're doing business on Sundays we're fined ten thousand dollars for every Sunday that they opened their doors. Christians even protested outside these stores when they opened, trying to discourage people from shopping on the 'Lord's Day'".

"Jake, I have with me Dr. Tim Dawson who is visiting in the area. Dr. Dawson is a recently retired Christian psychologist and internationally known figure in Christian circles. Dr Dawson has had a family-based ministry for many years and has been outspoken on moral issues since the early eighties. He has authored many books on parenting, marriage, and the family. Dr. Dawson, you stated to me earlier that this recent Sunday law is for 'societies own good'. Why do you say that?"

"Well, I don't like to get involved in politics or use my influence to sway people's minds one way or the other, but I am greatly concerned with today's issues, both in the physical world and in the political arena. It is obvious to me that the disasters and economic crisis that we find ourselves in today are due, as the President has said, to the greed of society and to families forgetting about God...and, I might add, treating Sunday like any other work day."

"So you agree with this law?"

"Today families go to church on Sunday, and then they are either working or they go to restaurants and malls or ball games. They have no quality time together. This, I believe, is why the divorce rate even among Christians is the highest that it has ever been in our nation's history. This has to change! I am convinced that God is trying to get our attention. We are supposed to be one nation under God. This recent Sunday law is a step in that direction, but we have a long way to go. As long as this nation continues killing the unborn child and legislating same sex marriage, and as long as Hollywood is allowed to promote pornography and openly opposes God and other moral imperatives, God's displeasure will be upon our country...and its people."[1]

"Thank you for your comments, Dr. Dawson."

# Chapter 6

"Daddy! Daddy!"

"My babies!! You're alive!"

"Are you okay?"

"Yes, Kimmy. The hospital is just keeping me here for observation. I'll be able to leave tomorrow. How are you?"

"OK! After we ran up the hill when you told us to, a helicopter with a strong man came down. He lowered this thing that wrapped around us. Then he picked us up and carried us up to the helicopter. We told the man about you and Mommy. Where is Mom?"

"I…I don't know, Kimmy. The rescuers haven't found her yet."

"But wasn't she with you?"

"We were separated, Honey. A tower came crashing down near us, and I held on to it until I was saved. I didn't see Mom after that."

"Mommy has to be safe because she prayed for Jesus to protect us. God wouldn't let her die, would He?"

"I'm not sure how to answer that right now! Let's just wait and pray." Both girls hugged their father, and they all started sobbing.

"According to the news there are survivors still being found. Most of the church members including many of your friends from school were saved. For now we'll be staying with church members until we get back on our feet. We must thank God for saving us and use our lives from now on to serve Him. The day the dam broke, a National Sunday law was passed. Many church groups are saying that it's the best thing for our society."

"What does that mean, Daddy?" asked Kimmy.

"It's a long story! There's so much I have neglected to tell both of you. Perhaps we could start with Matthew 24. Here Jesus is telling us what to expect before He returns. This chapter talks about wars, famines, earthquakes and other disasters, just like we've experienced and seen on the news. It even tells us that it's going to get worse for many in the churches, and for Christians in name only and non-Christians, and how people will become colder towards others."

"Like that man that got out of the car and started beating up the driver of the car that hit him?"

"Yes, that's one example of what this means."

"How do people get like that, Daddy?" asked Kimmy.

"Well, there are different reasons why people's hearts become cold. One reason is because of bad TV shows. These shows portray a lot of violence, crime, guns, bad music, immorality and other things that put bad thoughts into people's minds. When people watch these shows day in and day out they become desensitized and hardened...they get used to watching these things. So much so that when they see something bad happening to someone, it doesn't affect them. This is why someone being beaten up on the streets of a big city is ignored by those passing by. They just let it happen without trying to stop it."

"Excuse me, Mr. Smith. If I could just get your blood pressure real quick, I'll be out of your way."

"Sure, Nurse. You're not in my way."

"Thank you."

"No problem! Okay, girls, where was I? Oh, yes! Also when kids or adults can go into a church or campus or other places and start shooting innocent people, you know that they are not in their right minds. Many have come from very dysfunctional homes. They are so used to lying, cheating, stealing, and being involved in very unhealthful practices that when they are crossed or can't have their own way, they lose control. It doesn't happen all at once. This is why it's so important to not let malice, hatred or bitterness overcome us.[1] If we do, it will take us captive, and we will become cold, hardened, and distrustful of those around us."

"Look at the red bird, Daddy, over there on the window sill?"

"Yes, Kimmy. That's a woodpecker with a long beak...very colorful! Girls, I'm afraid that all of the godless teachings in our schools have turned society into humans that act like animals without a conscience.[2] Evolution has taught them that this is the only life there is. As far as the conscience goes, they say that there is no right or wrong...no absolutes. Everyone must choose what truth is for themselves, they say. In one of those magazines on the table over there I read an article that said that even among Americans—including those who describe themselves as 'born again Christians'—sixty-four percent of adults and eighty-three percent of teenagers say that truth is always relative to the persons and their circumstances. Only six percent of teenagers say that truth is absolute.'[3] Not much room for God or His law in those statistics."

"How many, Dad?"

"Six percent, Shannon."

"Wow! That's hard to believe. I'm glad I'm in the six percent."

"Yes, Shannon, me too! The majority deny the clear teachings of the Bible that are opposed to what the article called "relativism".[4] This falsehood, combined with the rejection of God by a large class in society, can be blamed on the confused doctrines of many churches. They teach that when we die, if we don't know God, we will go to hell where we will burn in a lake of fire throughout eternity. This teaching makes God look like a monster."

"Don't they know that's not in the Bible?"

"It doesn't appear that they do, Shannon! Otherwise I doubt they would be teaching or believing it. All I know for sure is that the Bible doesn't support this teaching. It teaches that when we die, we rest in the grave (Jesus likened it to sleeping) until the resurrection, when the dead in Christ and all the living and those who crucified Him will see Him return. Then after that we will be judged according to what our lifestyle choices were. Those who rejected Christ will suffer the punishment of hellfire and will be burned up completely including the devil and his angels."[5]

"This makes more sense to me than the teaching that says God will burn them forever without end. I couldn't imagine you or Mom punishing us forever for something we did wrong. You punish us according to what we did. Like that time I stole a cookie that Mom made for dessert. You didn't spank me for several hours. You only sent me to my room early."

"Exactly, Kimmy! And this is how God treats lost sinners. He will punish some less than others, depending on how bad they were. Well, we've covered a lot of ground. But we need to rest now, girls. We've been through a lot."

# Chapter 7

Hours later a sheriff walked into the room with his head hanging. Instinctively John knew why he was there. He had a gut-wrenching feeling as the Sheriff looked at him hesitantly.

"Not Lisa! Please, God!" John cried out. "Not Lisa!!"

"I'm so sorry, Mr. Smith."

"Daddy? Daddy!?! Is Mommy dead?"

"I, I, I'm—"

"Yes," the sheriff interjected, seeing that John was having a hard time saying it. "I'm so sorry—your mother didn't make it." He explained some of the details to the family.

"Why, Daddy? Mommy prayed for God to protect us all? Why didn't God protect and save her like He did us? It's His fault! I, I—"

"Please, Kimmy, don't say it!"

"I'm so sorry, girls!" the sheriff responded.

As the children began to cry, John said under his breath, "God, help me understand why you didn't save Lisa. How could you allow this?"

Some time after the sheriff left, Pastor Sven walked through the doors. "I'm so glad you're all okay."

"Not all. Lisa didn't make it. Her body was found yesterday."

"I am so sorry. I can only imagine how hard this is on all of you. Could we pray together?"

"Alright, Pastor"

After a short heartfelt prayer, during which the sobs of the children began to subside, Pastor Sven suggested, "Can I contact your other kids and family members for you?"

"Thanks, Pastor. That would be a blessing. I'll give you their numbers. I suppose they will need to have advanced notice so they can make it for the memorial service. It will be a long drive for some of them—Pastor Sven! *Why*?!? Why did God not save Lisa like He did us? I don't understand!"

"Yeah! Why did God kill my mommy? It's His fault."

"Kimmy!"

"It's alright, John. I don't mind if she expresses how she feels. This is natural. I felt the same way a long time ago when my first wife and six month old child were killed in an automobile accident by a drunk driver. He walked away without a scratch."

"I never knew you had another wife before Joanne!" John admitted to the pastor.

"Yes, it was very difficult for me to cope at the time. But eventually God blessed me with Joanne—and three wonderful kids. Two of them are serving the Lord in the ministry. It was like Joanne and I were made for each other. Time heals all wounds. Not that I have forgotten, but it's as if God stepped in and overruled the situation."

"I don't want another mother! I want my mommy! Why did God take my mommy?"

"I'm so sorry, dear! I can't give a definite reason why God allowed your mommy to be taken away from you. Perhaps explaining the little bit that I have learned over the years will give you some comfort. Kimmy, this is a question that God's people, including myself, have struggled with since the beginning of sin. WHY? If God is love, why is there so much pain and suffering? Why do innocent people suffer when so much of it appears to be senseless?"

"Pastor, I can understand why God allows bad people to die, but why my mother? I need my mother."

"I don't know, Shannon, but I want to assure you that I, my family--your whole church family--are hurting with you and all the others who lost loved ones. In 1 Corinthians 12:26 it says that when one member of the body suffers, we all suffer. We will all be here helping you through this difficult time. I want to share a Bible promise with you. The Scripture tells us that Satan comes to 'steal, kill and destroy, but I have come [says Jesus], to give them life—more abundantly.'[1] Ever since Satan got kicked out of heaven, he has looked for ways to get back at God. And the most successful way that he does this is to hurt (or even destroy) the apple of His eye, one of His children."

"Why was Satan kicked out of heaven?" asked Kimmy.

"I'll tell you. There was a war in heaven."

"A war?" Kimmy blurted out. "But I thought God hated war!"

"God does hate war and He tried to prevent it from happening. God had an angel called Lucifer who was in charge of all the other angels in heaven. The Bible says in Ezekiel 28 that he was the covering cherub. He was very beautiful and perfect in every way, with every precious stone covering him. He was the music director of heaven, too. Do you know what other talents were given him?"

"No! What?" she asked anxiously.

"Well, his 'pipes' were specially designed. This means he could sing alto, base, baritone, tenor, soprano…all at the same time."

"Wow, a one man show!" responded Kimmy.

"Lucifer knew that he had talent and eventually his head started to swell. So much so that he started feeling more and more that he deserved to have a higher position."

"But who had a higher position than he did? Didn't you say he was in charge of all the angels?"

"Yes! There wasn't any higher position—other than the one the Creator God held. So Lucifer had a real problem, didn't he?"

"I'll say he did," she agreed. "So what did he do next?"

"Lucifer knew that he couldn't just come out with his true feelings, so he had to come up with a subtler plan."

"Is that when God kicked him out of heaven?"

"No, God didn't kick him out yet. Even though God could read Lucifer's heart, He is very patient. He didn't want to kick Lucifer out. He allowed him to do what he did because He wanted to give him every opportunity to give up his foolishness. Unfortunately, girls, Lucifer continued scheming until he came up with a plan. Can you guess what that plan was and how Lucifer tried turning all the angels against God?"

"Uh, did they try firing missiles at Him?"

"Ha-ha! Well, in a manner of speaking, Shannon, I guess that's what Lucifer did, but not with physical missiles. Let me ask you a question: Did you ever have anyone tell a lie about you? And then continue adding to it until it got out of control and everybody believed the lie—when you knew it wasn't true?"

"Yes, not long ago a girl in church school started spreading rumors about me. She said things that really hurt."

"Were they true?"

"No! Not at all!"

"Why do you suppose the girl said all those nasty things about you?"

"Both of us were running for class president and when she saw that most of the kids wanted me, she started telling lies about me. Do you remember, Dad, when I came home crying because of all the lies that were going around school and church about me?"

"Yes, Honey, I remember."

"So how did you respond to those lies?"

"As much as I wanted to fight for my rights, I didn't. I know that Jesus doesn't want us to speak evil against anyone or to attack them because He suffered for us all. Jesus never got angry or attacked those who spoke evil against Him. Instead He allowed Himself to die on the cross for them."

"That's right, Shannon, and so true. Did you end up becoming class president?"

"At first the other girl got a lot more kids on her side. But when the teacher found out about the lies, he tried talking to the other girl about confessing her wrong doing."

"So did she?"

"No, instead she started talking bad about the teacher and how he was against her."

"So then what did the teacher do?"

"After being patient with this girl and still seeing no change in her attitude, he told the class about the lies that were said about me, just before the vote was to take place for class president."

"Then what happened?"

"The girl started screaming, 'Unfair! This is unfair!!' She got so out of control that the teacher had to send her to the principal's office, and she was suspended from school for a week. And, yes, I ended up becoming class president."

"Was it worth it all?"

"Yes, it was! Although the pain is still there somewhat, I *have* forgiven her. I even made some cookies and left them for her on her desk at school with a little note inside telling her how I wish we could be friends."

"You are following Jesus' counsel by loving your enemies and heaping coals on their head. You must not stop praying for her. As you were telling me this story, I couldn't help think how the principles involved were very similar to what happened in heaven with the great controversy between Christ and Satan."

"How so?" asked Shannon.

"Lucifer knew that God was his Creator and that God had all of the angels' allegiance. So since Lucifer's only chance of ascending higher would be to take God's position, he would need to get an army on his side in order to overthrow Him."

"How would Lucifer ever be able to turn the angels against God?" As the pastor had hoped, the children had temporarily forgotten their grief in the light of unfolding truth.

. "Shannon, I'm glad you asked that! Do you remember how your classmate, who was running for class president, got most of the students over to her side?"

"Yes, she started rumors and lies to cause the other kids to distrust me."

"Exactly. And Lucifer did the same thing!"

"How did he do that? How could Lucifer turn the angels against God? I mean, God is perfect, without any flaws."

"Yes, I know. This is where the story gets really interesting. You see, Lucifer started to plant seeds of doubt in the angels' minds. He gave them the impression that God had so many rules because He didn't trust them to make their own decisions. When Lucifer did what he did I can picture the angels who were loyal to God saying 'NO, NO, that isn't true—Is it?'"

"Yes!" sneered Lucifer. "I mean, think about it, why does God have so many rules? Doesn't He trust you?"

"Well…you do have a point, I suppose," remarked many of the angels.

"Sure I do," responded Lucifer. "True freedom and happiness shouldn't have so many rules should it? God is just trying to control you."

Knock, knock!

"Come in." interrupted John.

"Mr. Smith, I just wanted to stop by your room to see how you're doing."

"Hello, Doctor. I'm better now that my children—and our pastor—are with me. Thanks for checking up on me."

"You're very welcome. Your test results look good. I believe you'll be ready to go home tomorrow."

"That's good news, Doctor. Thanks for all you've done."

"I'm glad to be of help. I also wanted to express my condolences on the loss of your wife. These are trying times for us all; my eldest son is still missing...In any case, if you have a problem develop after you leave, feel free to call my office."

"Yes, sir, thank you. We'll be praying for your family! Sorry, Pastor. Please continue. Your story is helping me to sort things out."

"As I was saying, Lucifer was accusing God of having a power issue! I can picture a conversation between Lucifer and the angels, 'I've thought this through' says Lucifer, 'and I have come up with a solution to this problem. I can offer you freedom from all these rules, [similar to the teaching today that says there are no absolutes] but in order to do that I need to be sitting where God is now.'"

"'How could you possibly think such a thing?' urged most of the angels. 'God does not have all these evil intentions or motives as you say. God has supplied all our needs and we have never lacked anything. If you try taking the place of God, there will inevitably be a war. And you can never expect to win.' Many angels, however, said, 'Yes, I believe Lucifer is right. God is not being fair. We need a new ruler in heaven'"

"Daddy, I have to go to the bathroom."

"Okay, Kimmy, shut the door behind you. Hurry, though, so the pastor can continue his story."

After a couple minutes Kimmy returned. "Okay, I'm ready."

"So Lucifer accused God of having too many rules," the pastor went on.

"'If God trusts us,' Lucifer questioned, 'then why does He have so many rules? Is God insecure? It seems mysterious.'"

"For the first time there was discord in heaven. God and the loyal angels pleaded with Satan to turn from his self-destructive course—but he would not listen, and God finally had to put a stop to it. And this is why the war in heaven took place. If Lucifer were allowed to continue his lies then no one would be safe. It talks about it in Revelation 12: 7-10, 'And there was war in heaven. Michael and his angels fought against the dragon, and the dragon and his angels fought back. But he was not strong enough, and they lost their place in heaven. The great dragon was hurled down--that ancient serpent called the devil, or Satan, who leads the whole world astray. He was hurled to the earth, and his angels with him.'"

"Pastor," interrupted John, "I have enjoyed your talk very much, but what does any of this have to do with why God saved us and not Lisa? And why does He allow so much evil in the world today? I mean, after all, He could put a stop to it, couldn't He?"

"Yeah, Pastor, why did God kill my mommy?"

"I was just giving you the background of where sin began and was going to tell you next why it has been allowed to go on for the last 6,000 years. You see, it was obvious that God was stronger than Satan. After all, He did win the war in heaven, didn't He?"

"Yes!" they all chorused.

"Okay, I have a question for you! Did you ever run across a bully in school who everyone was afraid to mess with?"

"Oh, yes!" as Shannon perked up.

"Did you ever hear someone go up to that bully and confront him, knowing he wouldn't have a chance if a fight started?"

"It did happen once that I know of. After the bully did him in, the other boy never said anything bad to him again."

"Why do you suppose that was?"

"Well, because he knew the consequences if he did stand up to him."

"Exactly my point," said the pastor. "You see even though God had won the war, he now had a new dilemma. The loyal angels who didn't follow Lucifer [who was now called Satan], had worshiped God because they loved and trusted Him. Having witnessed God's almighty power, perhaps in the future they would worship Him out of fear.

"I see what you mean," responded Shannon.

"If the doubts that Satan tried to instill in their minds of God's justice did arise, they might think they wouldn't stand a chance if they questioned God. But He doesn't want His creation to worship him out of fear; He wants their worship to be voluntary, reasonable, loving! God had to show the universe that Satan's claims were false and that it was Satan and not Himself that had the evil plan to control the universe.

Satan's plan was to steal, kill, and destroy.[1] God had to let the angels and mankind see that He had their best interests in mind. The only way to do this was to let Satan's true ugliness be unmasked. Satan's deception of the human race started in the Garden of Eden."

"Could you explain that?" requested Shannon.

"Sure! In the garden, God gave Adam and Eve everything they could possibly desire. God did, however, give them a test. This was just a very small test to show whether or not they would be loyal to God or choose to believe Satan's lies. Disbelief of God's Word by eating of the forbidden tree was in effect rejection of His authority. When they did this they showed that they were distrusting God by yielding to appetite. Satan convinced our first parents that God was withholding good from them, and when they made the decision to believe him, they accepted Satan's rule over their lives. Since that time, man has been under the dictatorship of Satan."

"I'm sorry to interrupt again, but would you like a drink of water, Pastor?"

"Sure, Shannon. Thanks!"

"God had said before sin entered the world, 'You are free to eat from any tree in the garden; but you must not eat from the tree of the knowledge of good and evil, for when you eat of it you will surely die.'[2] Then later Satan came along and said 'You will not surely die.'[3] That was a bold-faced lie. But because they believed Satan, mankind has been suffering ever since. Satan's true character was revealed even more fully when he put our Lord and Savior Jesus Christ on the cross."

"I thought it was the religious leaders and the Romans who put Him on the cross."

"Well, yes, but it was Satan that inspired them to do it, Kimmy."

"Oh!"

"And it was at that point that the on-looking universe discerned Satan's true character. What to Satan seemed his greatest victory, ended up becoming his greatest defeat. Now the world is without excuse. It is seen that Satan's idea of freedom is in reality slavery. Listen to this statement from my favorite author. 'The fall of our first parents broke the golden chain of implicit obedience of the human will to the divine. And now obedience has no longer been deemed an absolute necessity. The human agents follow their own imaginations which the Lord said of the old world was evil and that continually.'"[4]

"Like at the time of Noah's flood?"

"Yes, Kimmy. God had power to hold Adam back from touching the forbidden fruit, but had He done this, Satan would have been sustained in his charge against Gods arbitrary rule. Man would not have been a free moral agent, but a mere machine.' 'It certainly was not Gods purpose that man should be sinful. He made Adam pure and noble, with no tendency to evil. He placed him in Eden, where he had every inducement to remain loyal and obedient. The law was placed around him as a safeguard.'"[5]

"So is this saying that all of Gods rules are to protect us and not to restrict our freedom?"

"Exactly, Shannon! It was because Adam and Eve chose to disbelieve God that we see all the pain and suffering in the world today. Adam and Eve experienced it firsthand when their very own son Cain challenged God. Cain believed that God was too strict in the method of sacrifice that He required to atone for sin. He figured he could offer just as good a sacrifice with fruits of the ground, but God said specifically that an animal sacrifice was required to pay for their sins. When God didn't accept Cain's sacrifice—and He did accept Abel's offering of a lamb—Cain became very angry. Abel tried to explain to Cain why his sacrifice wasn't accepted by God, but Cain couldn't be reasoned with and he 'attacked his brother Abel and killed him.'"[6]

"He did all that just because he was angry?" asked Shannon.

"Yes, he did! Do you see why Cain was so angry though? He was trying to save himself by his own works, apart from God's requirements. He thought he could offer a better way, but when things didn't work out, Cain couldn't control his anger. Are you watching the development here, girls? The same traits of character that originated in Satan are being repeated in the human race. If God had somehow forced Cain not to kill his brother then his worship of Him would also be a forced obedience, thus validating Satan's claim that God wants to control us."

"So does God leave mankind to himself now?"

"I'm glad you asked that, Shannon. I once read an inspired quote that explains it well. It says, 'When the curse was pronounced upon the earth and upon mankind, in connection with the curse was a promise that through Christ there was hope and pardon for the transgression of God's law. Although gloom and darkness hung, like the pall of death, over the future, yet in the promise of the Redeemer, the Star of hope lighted up the dark future. As soon as Adam sinned, the Son of God presented Himself as surety for the human race.[7] When Jesus died on the cross, He saved mankind from destroying themselves by 'averting the doom pronounced upon the guilty.' That's why we can leave our sins at the foot of the cross! "[8]

"So the reason Jesus died, Pastor, was to keep us from destroying ourselves?"

"Yes, Shannon! And it was our first parents' decision to go against God—and believe Satan's lie—that brought so much pain, suffering and death on this earth. After six thousand years of sin, we have seen the 'freedom' that Satan has to offer us for going against God's government and His law."

"Some freedom!" Kimmy blurted out.

"God wants His creation to see firsthand that His law 'was placed around him as a safeguard.'[9] And if we break His law we must experience the consequences. There is one commandment that recognizes God as the Creator of heaven and earth. But Satan, as we have seen from the beginning, wants to take the place of God and sit upon His throne to be worshiped."

"If the commandment already shows us that God is the Creator, then how can Satan change that?" asks Shannon.

"He did it by *seemingly* changing the law of God, that's how! But let me explain about that later because I really need to leave now. I have a Bible study in a few minutes and it's across town. The roads are still pretty bad in places; it can be slow going. John, I'm so glad that a family from the church in Little Rock is going to let you folk stay with them until you get back on your feet."

"Thanks, Pastor. You've given us a lot to think about."

"Keep in touch! And again, if there is anything I can do to help, just call me."

# Chapter 8

"Stay away from here, Pastor Sven."

"Please, Michelle, I know you were already hurting over your mother's recent death, and now your father—lost in the flood! It's horrible! I feel your pain."

"You don't know nothing! I don't want nothing to do with you—or your God!!"

"I'm not going to try to force you to listen to me, but I just want you to know that I'm here for you if you want to talk." After the pastor left, Michelle, who was staying at her Aunt's home, totally lost control and started throwing objects at the wall and crying hysterically.

Once back in his car, the pastor prayed that God would comfort and protect Michelle, that the "scales would be taken off her eyes" so she could see that God wasn't to blame for all the pain in her life. He also pleaded that she would give her battered heart to Jesus before it was forever too late! As he started the car to head for his next appointment, the radio broke in on his thoughts.

*"...twelve consecutive weeks of blistering, record-setting heat and no precipitation. We interviewed Alan Johns this morning as he returned from a tour of his one-thousand-plus acre farm just outside of Muskogee, Oklahoma.*

*"I'm tellin' you, if we don't get some relief in the next few weeks, we're done—the crops, the animals, even the machinery—it's just plain brutal."*

*"For Foss News! On the Road in the Midwest, I'm Linda Cochran."*

ೋ

A year or so later the Smith family had settled in the country outside of Little Rock. John got a call from his boss, Fred Johnson, on his cell phone.

"Hello, John. I need to speak with you in my office concerning an urgent matter."

"Sure, Fred. Let me finish showing Les how to fill out this contract on the Rogers' windmill sale, and I'll be right there."

As John entered the office a little later, a look of concern clouded Fred's face.

"John, you have been with this company for over fifteen years, and you have worked your way up to Regional Manager. You have helped build a positive image for our company. As a result of your dedication, we have received the Super Green Award as the highest producing company of energy saving products in the nation. I believe that God has been blessing our company because of you. Especially since the tragic loss of your wife and your home, you have become a more honest and ethical employee. Even though I know you work fewer hours in order to spend more time with your children, your sales have not suffered. As a matter of fact, as energy costs have skyrocketed, so have your sales! But I didn't call you into my office just to pat you on the back." Fred sighed deeply. "John, a federal law has just been passed..."

"A law?" John asked. "What kind of law?"

"This is hard for me, John! The new law requires employers to report employees who do not honor Sunday as a day of worship."

"Fred, do you remember I was telling you about the prophecies recently?"

"Yes, but I didn't believe it would go this far. Actually, I thought you were a little extreme in what you said—but I don't anymore! The media are condemning Sabbath keepers, just as you said they would. As a matter of fact, the other day an angry mob burned down a Sabbath-keeping Baptist church that was near my home. I couldn't believe it! There weren't very many who attended there anymore; the majority of them have switched over to Sunday keeping. So if I report you to the authorities, I'm afraid I'm going to lose you. I don't know what to do. To tell you the truth, I also fear for my life and the lives of my family. With all the foreclosures and unemployment, the streets are not safe anymore. It seems everyone is angry, and they're looking for someone to blame."

"I agree, Fred!"

"We've had our Bible studies together. I've read the 'Great Controversy' and other books you have given me that explain about this time in earth's history. And now I see the exact things happening that we've been studying about. Public opinion is turning against Sabbath keepers. They're being blamed for all the problems because of their stubbornness in keeping Saturday and refusing to worship on Sunday—even to save our society. I was surprised by the violent persecution here in the South—the Bible Belt, mind you! But ministers everywhere (including my own) are tearing Sabbath keepers apart, calling them the *worst* of the cults."

"Where do *you* stand?" John questioned.

"Well, when I approached my minister and asked him for biblical evidence, he went over the same weak arguments that we've already covered. When I questioned him on Saturday vs. Sunday using the Scriptures[1], he got very angry and stormed away. He hasn't been able to biblically prove that the Sabbath was changed from Saturday to Sunday. What should I do, John?"

"It's not what I think that counts."

"Let me finish your thought: It's the Bible that we should go by."

"Exactly!"

"I know by now that you don't accept tradition as your guide. *Sola Scriptura*—the Bible and the Bible only."

"Your answer is found in Joshua 24:15. 'Choose for yourselves this day whom you will serve.' Only you can make that decision. Do you wish to hold the popular opinion of worshiping on Sunday, a day that was ordained by man? Or do you wish to serve God on the day He sanctified, hallowed and blessed? [2] But really the controversy between Christ and Satan is not just over a day. It proves whose side we are on—who we pledge allegiance to! [3] This is why the issue over Saturday and Sunday is heating up more and more. This is Satan's final offensive in the war that began in Heaven—to show himself supreme and to try to get everyone great and small to worship him. Times are serious!"

"I'm seeing that now, John—more and more."

"'We are nearing the close of this earth's history.' 'Satan is making desperate efforts to make himself God, to speak and act like God, to appear as one who has a right to control the consciences of men.'[4] That's the reason it's getting harder all the time to buy and sell as Satan uses every evil tactic to get us to accept Sunday as the day of worship. It's almost impossible to worship in churches anymore. Because of the attacks on them, our insurance companies have ceased insuring our buildings, not only in response to recent laws, but also because of all the fires and vandalism. We cannot continue sustaining the loss. In most cases we have to meet in homes. Citizens of this community are even attacking Sabbath keepers on the street."

"How's your courage, John?"

"Well, I'll be honest, it's difficult. As you know, we moved into the country after the first Sunday law was passed. I knew that soon it wouldn't be safe in the city. We even started growing our own food on our small farm. My girls are good little gardeners; it's part of their homeschooling program. Since our private schools have been shut down, I've been teaching them at home. It's just impossible to send them to public school—their liberal agenda—teaching children evolution and ridiculing God's authority. If anyone dares to go against these teachings, the persecution gets ugly in a hurry! So I have been forced into homeschooling. I've never regretted it for a moment though. Soon the Sunday law will be so restrictive that it will be impossible to leave the cities. I've heard that in many larger cities this is already the case, especially here in the Bible Belt."

"Yes, John, I can see—"

"Mr. Johnson!" his secretary suddenly interrupted on the intercom, "A U. S. Marshall just rushed by me and is headed for your office—fast! I tried to detain him, but he wouldn't listen! I'm sorry…"

# Chapter 9

Seconds later the Marshall slammed opened the door and entered the room. Looking John's way, as if he already knew who he was, he asked gruffly, "Are you John Smith?"

"Yes, sir, I am. What's the trouble, Officer?"

The Marshall abruptly grabbed John's arms and handcuffed him. "Come with me!" he commanded.

"What is this?" asked Fred.

"Mr. Johnson, we need to question Mr. Smith at headquarters. My advice to you is to not get involved. If Mr. Smith is cooperative, he has nothing to worry about."

"What has he done to deserve this cruel treatment?"

"Don't ask any more questions!"

The Marshall dragged the unresisting John outside and threw him into a military van with three other prisoners. As they headed out into the country, John noticed many road signs that were unfamiliar to him. Eventually they stopped at the gate of what appeared to be a high security prison somewhere in the middle of the National Forest. As they proceeded through the gates, John observed that there were armed guards everywhere.

"So this is where all our tax dollars are going!" whispered one of John's fellow prisoners.

"I heard that," said the guard. "What should it matter to you? You don't believe in paying taxes, carrying a license, or supporting the government in any way. Remember? That's why you're here. You patriots can only run and try to hide from us for so long. Eventually you'll end up here because you refuse to obey the laws of the land. Did you actually think you could outsmart the government?"

"I won't support this government with my tax dollars. This government is Babylon!" retorted the indignant prisoner.

"Shut up," the guard yelled and hit the prisoner on the back of the head with the butt of his gun. As blood flowed from an ugly wound, he slumped to the floor of the van—unconscious.

Next John saw a large black helicopter maneuver itself sideways, then backwards, and land expertly on the roof. Uniformed guards hustled several handcuffed people out of the chopper and into the night. John was fighting anxiety, while all the time praying silently for God's protection. His first concern was for his girls, but he also now hoped for an opportunity to witness to this patriot—to share with him the message of Revelation 14, the *truth* about Babylon.

Soon they went through another gated area, then through two wide doors that silently swung open. The walls appeared to be several feet thick. Some kind of security bunker, he guessed. John was getting the distinct impression that he had been brought there for more than just questioning. Shortly the van pulled into a third gated area with a barbed wire fence all around it. The driver stopped and the guards stepped out, "Follow us. No talking." They set out down a long corridor, as quickly as they could while dragging the limp form of the patriot. John was having a hard time adjusting to breathing in the damp and musty-smelling air. After many turns and several checkpoints, they finally came to a solitary cell. The door opened electronically, and John was shoved inside. Ominously, the door slid shut and locked with a hollow click.

"Do I need an attorney?" asked John.

The guards look at each other and laughed darkly.

"I know my rights, gentlemen. As a citizen of the United States, I have the right to call my attorney."

"Not today you don't," said one of his captors in heavily accented English. As they walked away, the guards start speaking in what sounded to John like a Southern European language.

After several weeks, John's health showed definite signs of deterioration. He was shivering and coughing, with deathly pale cheeks and sore teeth due to the dampness of his cell and the meagerness of the food supply. John was nearly delirious by the time a guard opened the door and growled, "Come with me." John had difficulty getting up and at first his legs refused to carry him. Eventually, with the guard's unwilling assistance, they made the torturous trip back through the maze of prison corridors. They entered a room where a uniformed man was sitting behind a large metal desk.

"Sir," John croaked in a hoarse whisper, "what is this place?"

"I will ask the questions!" answered the Warden. "What is your name?"

"Before I answer any questions, I would like my attorney to be present. The United States Constitution allows me that right. You have held me in this damp prison, where I have been treated worse than a wild beast, without representation or any formal charges, in violation of my rights as a citizen."

"Terrorists who plot against our country and who have committed hate crimes do not have the protection of the Constitution," snapped the warden, "Now SHUT UP—and answer my question!"

"Wait a minute—What do you mean when you say I'm a terrorist? I love my country! This must be a case of mistaken identity."

"Do you keep Saturday as your Sabbath?"

"Well, yes." answered John with a puzzled look.

"Then that proves that you are a terrorist!" boomed the warden. "You and others like you are the cause of all the disasters around the world. You have been plotting with others and distributing hate literature that has been banned, like 'The Great Controversy' and other subversive books that speak against the Sunday law that our nation has put in place in order to save our country. Now the United States is threatened with bankruptcy and natural disasters are spiraling out of control—and it's all because of you Sabbath keepers."

"Why do you say Sabbath keepers are at fault for these problems?"

"Because they are in violation of the laws that have been set up to bring God's blessing back on our land—but He can't because you apostates refuse to worship on the Lord's Day. And because you are violating the Sunday Law, His frown is still upon us and we are suffering a National meltdown. Therefore, it is better that Sabbath keepers pay the price for their rebellion, than that the whole nation perish.[1] What do you have to say for yourself?

"I don't understand, Warden, What does any of this have to do with Sabbath keepers?"

"It's because you stubbornly persist in keeping Saturday as the Sabbath? Your Bible says that you are to obey the civil authorities, does it not? Don't you know that the old Sabbath was done away with at the cross? We true Christians honor the Lord now on Sunday because that is when Jesus rose from the dead. Since the first Sunday law passed you apostates are going everywhere telling the world that Sunday worship is the 'Mark of the Beast'. That's a hate-crime of the worst sort. Why do you speak such nonsense? The churches and the governments are working together to bring crime under control and legislate God's laws so that our country will return to its Christian roots. Do you know how long and hard the Christians, particularly the Roman Catholics, have worked to unite the church with the state. It's an ecumenical movement. But you Sabbath keepers are fighting against everything we do. Look at all the problems David Koresh caused. You're just as bad as he was—if not worse. Are you willing to cease and desist from your subversive activities for the sake of our families and our nation?"

John darted a quick prayer to heaven and began his defense. "Sir, I want you to know that I love my country. And so do all those who are anticipating Christ's soon return. We have been grossly misrepresented in the media. We are not extremists or fanatics. We're not at all like David Koresh or others out there who believe that the government is their enemy. We are tax-paying citizens. I served in the armed forces for fifteen years to defend the liberties our nation has stood for. Our position as the most favored nation in the world is built upon liberty of conscience. I believe that one reason, among many, that God has blessed our nation so much in the past is because we had a Constitution that allowed everyone freedom of religion."

"Wait a minute," the Warden interrupted. "What do you mean 'in the past?'"

"Our nation" responded John "became what it was because of the Christian principles that it stood for."

"Exactly!" retorted the warden. "That's what we want to go back to, but you Sabbath keepers are preventing us from being united because of your cultist activities."

John continued, "The story of the founding of Christianity in America is the record of true pioneers. The New World provided a haven for oppressed Christians from Europe. Several groups came to America to find a place where they could worship God according to their convictions and in peace—a freedom only dreamed of in Europe. John Winthrop, the first governor of the Massachusetts Bay Colony said about this nation, 'We shall be as a city upon a hill. The eyes of all people are upon us; so that if we deal falsely with our God in this work we have undertaken and so cause Him to withdraw His protection from us, we shall be made a story and a by-word through the world.'"[2]

"The first governor of Massachusetts said that?"

"Yes, Sir. We believe in freedom of worship just as the forefathers of this nation did. We do not believe in promoting or enacting civil penalties for those who do not worship the way we do—or their enforcement by civil power. God alone is worthy to be served. Enforcing religious laws does not make a person or a nation Christian. God seeks worship of the heart, and governments cannot make a person a Christian inwardly by enforcing laws. And they are, in effect, attempting to take God's place when they do. The state cannot decide for me how to worship—or not worship—God. This goes against everything our nation was founded upon.[3] It is the enforcement of Sunday Laws that has brought God's wrath on this nation to a point where her cup of iniquity is almost filled up. Sabbath keepers love this nation so much that they are warning our government—and their neighbors, their friends, their co-workers—that if they continue to violate God's laws, then God's judgments inevitably will be poured out upon them."

"How do you know all this?" asked the warden, this time a little less forcefully. The Holy Spirit was working mightily on the heart of this honestly deluded man.

"God's Word tells us! It tells us that if we worship the beast and have his 'mark', God's wrath will be poured out upon us. God is calling a people out of Babylon."[4]

"What are you talking about? What does all this have to do with our nation enforcing Sunday Laws? We are only trying to bring God's favor back to us and to save our families."

"Enforcing religious laws will not bring deliverance. You cannot legislate morality. This President once said that we have become a materialistic society that is greedy and immoral. I must agree. Things once detested by our nation have now become idols to us. With the passage and enforcement of Sunday Laws, our nation has rejected the God of Creation and accepted Satan's ruler-ship and agenda.[5] However, those who accept and serve the God of Creation and keep His Commandments have God's Seal and Mark of ownership.[6] The rewards of serving God instead of accepting this 'image of the beast' are peace and happiness! And we will reign with Christ forever."

After further discussion of these and other Bible teachings, a rather subdued warden called the guard and instructed him, "Take Mr. Smith and put him in another cell—and see that he receives better care."

# CHAPTER 10

When John did not return to work following his arrest, Fred started checking out all of the known prison facilities. He couldn't locate John's whereabouts, so he started calling members from John's church to see if they had heard from him. He had the strong impression that this was the time that John had told him about when God's commandment keepers who went against the false system of worship would be fined, imprisoned, and some, John had told him, would even receive the death sentence. Fred wondered if John were still alive? He knew that John—and others—had already been fined for speaking out against the abuses that were becoming so common. The law classified it as a hate crime, and they had been warned to desist from their divisive activities. Many were even calling them terrorists. This worried Fred.

"Excuse me, Mr. Johnson," his secretary interrupted his disquieting thoughts, "There's a phone call for you."

"Take a message for me, if you would, Nyla. Thanks."

Fred continued to ponder. He knew that if a Christian were convicted of terrorism, that it was considered treason, punishable by the most inhumane death possible (as an example to those tempted to follow him). Finally Fred couldn't take it anymore, and he broke down crying. "Dear God!" he prayed, "Everything is happening just as John said it would. 'The Great Controversy' is being fulfilled before my very eyes. Forgive me, God, for hesitating because of my family and church. I was wrong. Lord, I know the consequences if I receive Your truth. But if I reject it, then I will receive the plagues. I'm scared, Lord! But I choose to give You my life completely, come what may." As Fred prayed this sincere prayer, a peace and a power that he had never experienced came over him. Suddenly, he got a deep impression that he should get John's girls out of their home as soon as possible. He left the office and rushed to do the Holy Spirit's bidding.

As he arrived at the Smith home, Shannon and Kim noticed the look of urgency on his face, and Kim asked, "Mr. Johnson, are you okay?"

"Yes, I'm alright, thank you! Girls, I know it's been several weeks since your dad was taken away, and you've been anxiously waiting for him to come home. But things have intensified since he was arrested and you need to leave your home—now! I'm here to take you to a safer place."

"But what about our farm—and my dad?" Kim's face crumpled. "What if he returns and can't find us?"

"Your dad is being protected by God's angels. He'll be okay. But we need to leave."

After traveling for several hours, Fred and the girls arrived at a rustic building surrounded by a dense forest. "This cabin is where my family and I come at times to get away. There's canned fruit and other staples in the pantry. It's been a while since we've been here, so it needs a little cleaning. Stay here until I come back for you. There's a Bayjun short wave radio in the drawer. You need to crank it sixty times to get it to work for half an hour. That way you can tell what's going on. But try not to use it too much. Government surveillance is capable of tracking you by picking up your signal."

"How do you know all this, Mr. Johnson?" asked Shannon.

"I was trained in the military. The law hasn't gotten super restrictive—yet—as far as tracking Sabbath keepers this way, but I expect that to change anytime. I'm going back to see if I can get my family. I just accepted the Truth, but they don't know about my decision. So pray that they will want to join me in it. I'm not going to mention that you are up here until I have a chance to talk with them, just in case they turn against me. There's enough food here for a few weeks. When knowledge of my decision gets out (and I'm already under suspicion!), I won't be able to buy food anymore. Known Sabbath keepers can't buy or sell at all; every day the laws are getting tougher. My national ID card will undoubtedly be deactivated. I have some basic supplies at home, so I'll bring what I can when I come back."

"Will you be okay, Mr. Johnson?"

"I'll be fine. It's just that it's all happening so rapidly. I think I will have enough gas for the round trip. If not, I might have to hike some. I do have a five gallon can full of gas in my garage. The bigger cities have checkpoints on all the main roads, so I don't know what's going to happen. If I don't return, trust Jesus and He will send His angels to feed you."[1]

Meanwhile, the three were unaware that government authorities had come to arrest Shannon and Kim shortly after Fred had left with them. Not being able to find them, they had ransacked the home and taken the animals.

As Fred headed home, the weather radio in his Cherokee announced a severe storm warning for a system capable of producing destructive wind velocities. Dark clouds began to shut out the sun and the sky took on a strange greenish cast. Then, in the distance, but moving rapidly toward him, Fred saw the storm's giant funnel cloud, destroying everything in its wake. He had barely enough time to whisper, 'Lord, save me!' before the full force of the storm was upon him. As he braced himself for the onslaught, now only several hundred feet in front of him, the funnel suddenly lifted and veered sharply south, already beginning to dissipate. He had never witnessed anything like this before. Totally shaken, he dazedly listened to the radio announcer's excited description of the damage that had been done.

*"Never before has Arkansas experienced what meteorologists are calling 'a land hurricane'. Just as it developed almost without warning, and seemed to be building into a mighty force of destruction, it was somehow robbed of its power. The only mute reminders left behind are the devastated areas where the funnel touched down. The storm's miraculous ending at the height of its fury, just moments ago, has our scientist's totally baffled! For Foss News! I'm Angela Morris."*

After the hurricane had passed, Fred sat in his vehicle recovering from the shock and marveling at his deliverance. This time his whispered prayer was, "Thank You, Jesus!" Back on the road again, he decided to switch to the Christian radio station out of Little Rock; perhaps there would be some soothing music to calm his shattered nerves. Instead, Dr. Tim Dawson, recently retired from Families in Focus, was addressing a large ecumenical rally in Washington, D. C., "...and we must stop these troublers of Israel. Our nation is suffering economic ruin because these Sabbath keepers are persistent in their rebellion against God. He is punishing us—and will continue to punish us—if we allow these people to live. We must push our Congressmen to pass laws, just as we did with the first Sunday Laws. Except this time they must be silenced once and for all. If the members of our churches unite and flood the Capitol Hill phone lines, fax machines, and emails until they see that we are of one mind, then change will come. I'm throwing all my influence behind this. Our Catholic friends are also joining hands to help us be, as a former President from the great state of Arkansas has said, the 'Repairers of the Breach.' My friends, now is the time to put aside our differences and unite to save our great country. God bless America!"[2]

"Oh, my!" Fred said to himself. "I have *got* to get home quickly—if I still have a home, that is! God help me to save my family from receiving the plagues that are coming." The aftermath of the storm was everywhere in evidence, but as Fred prayed, thoughts came to him of what streets were safe to take. He arrived home to see torn up outbuildings, twisted, fallen trees, and general disorder. The main house seemed intact, however. "Praise the Lord!" Fred breathed. His wife and kids came running out to meet him.

"Fred, where have you been?" asked his wife Jackie.

"Daddy, we were worried about you. We were afraid that you might have been caught in that awful storm. We couldn't get a hold of you on your phone."

"I'm okay! We're all safe now. I just had to take care of some urgent business." Fred and the family went inside. While he showered and changed clothes, he prayed for the Holy Spirit to give him the right words—and the right timing—to share his convictions with his precious loved ones. He came back downstairs and said to his family, "I have some very important news to share with you after supper."

"Why, you're shaking, Fred! What's the matter?" asked Jackie.

"It's been quite the day, Honey." After the family had eaten, Fred asked them all to come into the living room so they could talk.

# CHAPTER 11

While his family listened in awe, Fred spent several minutes explaining his new found experience and the incredible happenings of the day.

After he finished Jackie spoke up, "I have a confession to make."

"You do?" responded Fred.

"Yes. For some time, I have been following the news and listening to the Christian radio station. The other night I was surfing the web and found a very interesting site called 3ABN—3 Angels Broadcasting Network, I think it stands for. They're Sabbath keepers. They were talking about counteracting the counterfeit. I'm not sure exactly what that means, but they seemed so…sincere…and loving! As court stenographer, I have also been present when Sabbath keepers from the Adventist church, as well as the Seventh Day Baptist churches, stood up in court to answer for their faith. The calmness that they had was incredible. Some former Adventists that we met when we went to John's church actually testified against the faithful members. Though they were facing the possibility of stiff sentences, through it all they seemed to have a peace that was a constant source of strength and courage. I couldn't help thinking that the former members were lying, their stories conflicted so often. It was just like Christ's trial. The testimonies of the witnesses didn't agree with each other. But, Fred, the Sabbath keepers were so serene. It really impressed me."

"Mom, a band on my braces just broke," interrupted their seventeen year old son Tyler.

"Okay, Tyler, go in the bathroom and see if you can fix it." his mother responded.

"Please continue!" John urged Jackie.

"Well, recently Pastor Sven had to appear before the court when a girl by the name of Michelle, a former member of their church, spoke against him. The Prosecuting Attorney was especially hard on him. You may find this hard to believe, but Attorney Campbell actually slapped him. In all my experience as a court worker, I have *never* experienced or even heard of such a breach of protocol in a state courtroom. And the judge said *nothing*; in fact, no one said anything to defend him. I was outraged by the whole trial. It was a mockery of justice. But through it all, the Pastor remained calm."

"He remained calm?" Fred questioned incredulously.

"Yes! It was amazing. Even though in my opinion the prosecution had nothing substantial enough for conviction—and after he showed that everything he believed was in the Bible—they still convicted him as a terrorist. I knew his response was supernatural. I had the strong conviction that God must be with him. When I talked to our Pastor, he said that Satan inspired the Adventists. I then remembered some of the conversations that Lisa and I had when we would go shopping. She told me of these things that are now taking place. I thought she was crazy, but now I see what she told me is true.[1] I wish so much that she were still alive so I could talk to her."

"It's okay, Honey. She's safe now awaiting the resurrection. At that time, all tears will be wiped away."

"I've been tossing a lot of things back and forth in my mind, and I'm fearful about our church's actions. Many of our members have lobbied against these Sabbath keepers and fought to silence them. At the same time, I'm fearful for us. I have seen where some of our church members who joined the Adventists have received fines, or have been sent to jail, or have just disappeared like John. To be honest, I also feared what your response would be, honey. Now I see that time is running out, and I remember how Lisa warned me of the plagues that are coming for all those who reject the truth and receive the 'mark of the beast'.[2] I don't want to receive that mark, Fred! I want to spend eternity with Jesus and my family."

"Mommy?" Their eight year old daughter had a question.

"Yes, Tara?"

"These people can't buy anything if they are Sabbath keepers, right? What will we do for food if *we* become Sabbath keepers?"

"'Jesus will take care of us, Sweetie! He promises that He will never leave or forsake us.'"[3]

"Why don't we pray?" suggested Fred.

"Just a second, Fred. Tyler, are you almost finished?" yelled his mom. "Tara, will you see what's taking your brother so long?"

"OK, Mom." When Tara checked the restroom, it was empty. Then she noticed that the back door was wide open.

"Mommy, I think Tyler's gone!"

"What?" yelled her daddy.

After several minutes of searching, the terrible premonition came to Fred that Tyler had joined forces with the enemies of God. "Quickly! We must leave—and right now."

"But honey, what about our son? We can't just leave him here. Please!"

"Jackie, I'm convinced that he's gone to turn us over to the authorities. We must leave—before it's too late!"

"My son, my son!"

"Honey, I'm so sorry. We can't turn back now."

"What about our other kids? Shouldn't we call them to see if they're okay?"

"I'm sorry, dear, we just don't have time. We will pray for them, but right now may be our only window of escape."

Meanwhile, Tyler was on his way to the police station.

As Tyler rushed into the lobby, the duty officer asked, "Can I help you, son?"

"Yes," he managed as he tried to catch his breath. "My name is Tyler Johnson." He fumbled for his wallet. "Here's my national ID card. I want to report some terrorists."

"Come with me please," the officer responded.

The two made their way to a back office. The duty officer returned to his post after assuring Tyler that someone would be with him shortly. As Tyler waited there, through the thin partition he heard the sounds of a struggle, then a deep commanding voice. "You don't seem to understand that I mean business! Tell me where those terrorists are…where are they?" yelled the interrogator. There came the loud sound of a slap, and then a woman's quiet sobbing. "You are a stubborn fool!" said the male voice. A door slammed. A sudden wave of conviction came over Tyler that he should stop what he was doing and turn back before it was too late. But he brushed the conviction aside and continued in his determination to betray his family.

The door to the office where Tyler waited opened and the precinct Sergeant came into the room. He apologized for keeping Tyler waiting. "I would have been here sooner, but I had some urgent business that I had to finish up. I understand you have some information for us."

Tyler recognized the voice of the interrogator, but he still refused to be swayed from his evil course. "Yes, sir, I do, but first I want to find out what the reward is for turning terrorists over to you."

"Are you referring to these Seventh-day Sabbath keepers?"

"Yes, sir."

"Very good! We do have substantial rewards. I took a quick look at your criminal history, and it appears you have a record. Tyler, I know how hard it can be to find a good job when you've had trouble with the law. Would you like it if that record could be cleared up?"

"Yes, sir! I sure would."

"Well, it's quite simple really. All you need to do for us is to give us the names and addresses of these terrorists. When they're convicted, your criminal history will be removed. Is that what you had in mind?"

"Yes, but since this involves my family, and I know a lot of details that I could give you, is there any *other* reward?"[4]

"There are special packages for those who turn state's evidence with insider information. If we get a successful prosecution, we can reward you financially as well. What did you say your age was?"

"I'm seventeen," responded Tyler.

"Since you are only seventeen, the government can grant you full emancipation as a minor, and we will also give you all that belonged to your family. How does that sound?"

"Great," responded Tyler. "I mean, anything that helps our wonderful Country…I'm all for that."

The Sergeant hesitated as if he were choosing his words carefully. "I've been thinking that perhaps you would like a job that pays *very* well?"

"Like what?" inquired Tyler.

"We are always looking for trustworthy informants. For every terrorist that you turn over to us that leads to a solid conviction, the government will pay you ten thousand dollars. Also, you will receive immunity from any crime committed against them in the line of duty. For instance, if they were *accidentally* killed in the process—if you know what I mean—the reward would still be yours. The way our kind-hearted President looks at it is that, if they are terrorists, they need to be silenced at any cost. So as far as we're concerned, you're not actually committing a crime, you're helping us save our nation. We don't offer this to just anyone, Tyler. But since you show such great loyalty and enthusiasm for the welfare of our country, not even letting family ties get in your way, we believe you are a real patriot and a real asset to our cause."

"I would love to help in any way I can," Tyler declared, the hint of a demonic smile playing on his lips.

"Very well, then. First off we need to pick up your family for questioning. Then we need to give you your next assignment."

In the meantime, the Johnsons rushed out of the house, jumped into the Jeep, and headed for their cabin. As they came to the outskirts of town, Fred realized that he had forgotten the gas can and the food.

"I'm almost out of gas. And in our rush to get out, I left the gas can and the food I meant to bring back at the house." Fred admitted.

"We're hardly out of the city. Should we go back and get it?"

"It's not safe anymore, Jackie. We'll need to trust the Lord! We need to pray, honey. Will you pray while I drive?"

"Sure! Jesus, you know our situation. You promise to supply all our needs. Please be with us in our dilemma and help us make it to the cabin. Amen!"

"Fred, there's someone up ahead on the side of the road; his car might be broken down or something. Should we stop and see if we can help?"

"I was just thinking that, but I'm a little nervous. Jesus *does* say that if someone is in need, we should help them."[5]

Fred decided to pull over. As he climbed out of the vehicle to offer assistance, the man said, "Fred, take your family in this Hummer and go to your cabin!"

"How did you know my name…and where we are going?"

"Don't ask questions. Just do as I suggest—there is no time to delay!"

"Jackie, Tara, come quickly!" As his wife and daughter were making the transfer, Fred turned to thank the stranger—but he was gone.

"Get into the vehicle."

"But Fred…!"

"I'll explain on the way."

As Fred explained what happened, Tara exclaimed, "Daddy! Was that an angel? This sounds like the stories we've heard about in Sunday school!"

"I believe it must have been, sweetie!"

"Wow! I've never seen an angel before!"

"Yes, Tara. Jesus promises us that He will send His angels to take care of us in our times of need."

"Fred, why do you suppose the angel supplied us with a Hummer? It seems to me that our Jeep would have brought us to our cabin just as well?"

"I'm not sure, Jackie. All I can say is God knows best."

As the family traveled deeper into the forest, there was increasing debris on the road. Finally, they came to a section that looked nearly impassable.

"Oh, no! Fred, there are trees down everywhere—even on the road. How will we…?"

"Don't worry. We can go around the trees with this Hummer. I guess this is our answer; the Jeep never would have made it."

"Praise God! I guess I shouldn't have questioned Him."

"The land hurricane must have come through this way, dropping trees wherever it touched down."

As the family approached the cabin and parked under the security light, Jackie noticed that there were bulk bags of grain, beans, dried fruit and nuts in the back of the Hummer. "Fred, take a look at this!"

"What's the matter?"

"Look! Praise God! He is so good!"

"What's going on?" Shannon asked, as she came out of the cabin.

After warm embraces from Shannon and Kim, Jackie said, "Shannon, the older you get, the more you look like your mother. And Kim, you have grown so much! I think it's been a year and a half since I last saw you girls...before you lost your mother. I'm just beginning to realize what a true friend she was!"

After much discussion of the recent events, Shannon said, "I'm sorry to hear about Tyler."

"Yes, it breaks my heart!" lamented Jackie. "Tyler never did have an interest in God. You might have heard that he was arrested not long ago for possession of a large quantity of drugs. He had an illegal weapon as well. He was out on bail, waiting to be tried as an adult. Still, I miss him so much."

"I really miss my mom since she died—and my dad since the Marshall took him. I hope he's okay." A tear trickled down Shannon's cheek.

"We must keep your dad, Tyler, your siblings, and our other kids in our prayers. It's not too late for them. 'Where there's Life, there's hope.' Let's stow this 'manna' and make some dinner. Then we can sing and study God's word together before bedtime prayers."

"At least *one* good thing has happened since the first National Sunday Law was enacted." responded Shannon. "I have had time to get closer to Jesus. I'm beginning to see why He allowed our family to go through everything that has happened. It was to prepare us for this time and to make our characters more like Jesus. Mom never could have made it with her health issues. I believe that's why she didn't survive the flood."[6]

"I'm thankful too," responded Kim. "If I hadn't gone through these tough times, I never would have known that I can trust God no matter what He chooses for my life. I can't wait to thank Him in person for what He has done. I understand now that it is Satan who has caused all the problems in this sinful world, while all along trying to get us to blame God. I still miss Mom—and I will until we are reunited in heaven—but I don't blame God anymore, like I did at first."

"With the way things are going, it won't be long before we see Jesus face-to-face" agreed Jackie. "I too have spent much time pondering my condition over the last year and a half, ever since that first Sunday Law. I'm glad I made a full surrender—and I want more than anything to continue to grow in my walk with the Lord."

After dinner and Bible study together, the weary group committed their lives once again into the keeping of their Heavenly Father and, with grateful hearts, went to bed.

The next day, Fred cranked the radio to hear the news.

"*...and the homes of suspected Sabbath-keepers are being confiscated throughout the country. Many of these terrorists have been* *caught trying to leave the cities. Rewards are being offered to anyone leading authorities to the whereabouts of those who the government has listed as threats to national security. Stay with Foss News! for updates of the War on Terror."*

"Did you hear that, Jackie?"

"Yes, Fred. We got out just in time! Praise the Lord!!"

"And it's just a matter of time before they come searching for us."

"But Fred, they don't know where we are."

"I hope you're right! My real concern is what Tyler might tell them."

"Surely our own son wouldn't betray us...would he?"

"Perhaps not, but the Bible does say that 'a man's enemies will be the members of his own household'.[7] The day Tyler left really opened up my understanding; the puzzle pieces began to fit together. The Spirit of the Lord is being withdrawn from the earth and everyone is taking sides.[8] When the Spirit of God is fully withdrawn, Satan will have complete control of those that worship the beast and his image. I remember John telling me that this will be Satan's last opportunity to recruit followers in his insane plan to win the war that started in heaven. Jesus' second coming puts an end to that—Praise the Lord!—and then comes the one thousand years that we are in heaven with Jesus. During that time, Satan and his evil angels are quarantined here on earth with no one to tempt because the wicked have all been killed by the brightness of His coming. After the millennium, we return from heaven and the wicked are resurrected, Satan rallies his troops to attack God and the New Jerusalem.[9] If he loses this war, and we know he will, then he, along with all his followers will be destroyed in the lake of fire.[10]

To say he's desperate is to put it mildly. I'm going to listen to the news now, Jackie. I'll take the Jeep and the radio and be back in a couple hours or so."

"Why so long, Fred? Why not listen to it here at the cabin?"

"Like I told Shannon, whenever a short wave radio is operating, the military can track the signal, just as they can with cell phones. I'm sure that the authorities are looking for us. This really is a war! I even heard that the people who are turning Sabbath keepers in are stealing their property the government is doing nothing to stop it. If children, who are under the legal age, turn their parents in, authorities are emancipating them and giving them all their family's property and possessions. We cannot be too careful!"

Several weeks passed and food supplies were running low. Fred and Jackie considered their options. They did the only the only thing that made sense: joined each other in prayer to seek God's direction. Angels drew near as sincere hearts petitioned a prayer-answering God.

# Chapter 12

"Tyler, your family wasn't at their home. Do you know where else they could have gone?"

"Hmmm," responded Tyler, "the only other place I can think of would be our cabin. It's up north of here."

"I doubt they could have made it that far without being observed," replied the sergeant. "We have roadblocks everywhere. The Highway Patrol briefings indicate that the land hurricane did extensive damage up that way. What kind of vehicle do they drive?"

"Jeep Cherokee."

"Nope, they never would have been able to get through with a Jeep. They would have needed a much larger vehicle to get through that—if it were possible at all."

"Do I still get my reward money?"

"Of course—as soon as they're in custody. And while we're searching for them, I do have another assignment for you. That is, if you'd still like to help us?"

"Sure. I would be glad to help; that is..."

"...if the price is right, eh? Don't worry; we'll make it worth your while. Anyway, there's someone here I'd like you to meet." The sergeant beckoned to a waiting officer. "Bring her in."

Moments later the door opened. "Tyler, meet Michelle. You two are going to be working together. Michelle is a former Adventist. Her parents were religious missionaries, but they're both dead now. She knows the Adventist lingo and can mingle with their group. She has been a highly successful operative, helping us find these traitors and picking up useful information. She even led us to the ringleader of the movement in this area, a Pastor Sven."

"I've heard of him," responded Tyler.

"Pastor Sven has been one of the most stubborn cases yet; so far we have not been able to persuade him to turn from his cultist activities. Another problem has developed, also. The Sabbath keepers have begun suspecting that Michelle is the one who is turning over the members to us. As a result, her sources have dried up and her usefulness as a field operative is about over. So this is where *you* come in. Michelle will give you the names of some of the members, and we want you to get the information that we need to round them up and secure convictions. Does that sound like something you would be willing to tackle??"

"Sure!" Tyler readily agreed. "But how am I supposed to get it?"

"We want you to go where Michelle tells you and act like you're interested in learning more about their beliefs—that's what they're looking for. Once you gain their confidence, we want you to start finding out all you can about them: everybody they know, where they're staying, friends, relatives, whoever and whatever might be useful to us. Okay?"

"Why can't I get more information if I just go directly to their churches?"

"The Adventists now meet secretly. We've taken control of their churches, their private school system, their entire infrastructure. They actually had a very organized movement. We have gained a great victory there. It was tricky to get the laws passed that we needed. But since the economy has gone down and we have so many other troubles in our nation, many people are willing like never before to give up their rights—even the protection of the Constitution. Still the Adventists stubbornly insist on meeting privately. So your part is to infiltrate and get us the information requested."

"Sounds good to me!"

"You need to be very cautious though. They're on their guard, so don't be too anxious to get the information all at once. And don't worry about money; we'll give you plenty. If you do good for us, the government will give you immunity for anything that becomes, uh, necessary. We need these troublers of Israel silenced so that Gods' blessing can be poured out on this nation once again. That's what God wants, and He's waiting for us to do our duty."

When Michelle gave Tyler the list of names, he said excitedly. "I can't wait to get at these people! Now's my chance to be the secret agent I've always wanted to be! My parents used to tell me that all my computer gaming would ruin my mind; instead it's prepared me for my future career in government!" said Tyler half-jokingly.

"Just be careful" warned the sergeant "and remember, don't be in too much of a hurry! We don't want this operation blown. Also we're giving you the code name Steven, so that you'll be harder to profile."

"Right," Tyler nodded.

Tyler was told in advance that Adventists 'pretend' to be very caring and concerned about the welfare of those around them, sharing their heresy with anyone who is willing to listen in order to win them to their side. He remembered this and carefully planned the approach of his first encounter. Having also been told that Adventists often go door-to-door sharing their beliefs, Tyler decided to make contact in a particular neighborhood where his subjects, Andrew and Laura Harris, were visiting homes to share their faith. As they were between houses, he casually walked up to them and asked, "You folks from around here?"

"No, we live a little ways from here! We're just giving some good news to those who want to listen."

"Good news about what? I could use some good news."

"The Good News about Jesus and His soon return!" confided Andrew.

"I've heard about some of these things!" said Tyler. "And I've been curious about what they meant. My name's Steven. I had been visiting some sick friends, when I saw you two, and you just seemed…well, different. Do you maybe have some time to talk?"

"Certainly!" responded Laura. "I'm Laura, and this is my husband, Andrew. Let's sit on that bench in the park." As they shared with Tyler, he pretended enthusiasm and a thirst for more spiritual information. Andrew and Laura were excited that they had found an interested soul, especially after having had doors slammed in their faces all day. Several hours of intense conversation followed. As they parted, Tyler set up an appointment with the Harrises for the next day.

"Isn't this exciting?" Laura beamed at Andrew. "Another soul for the kingdom!"

After a few more weeks of regularly meeting together, the three had gotten to know a lot about each other; a bond of friendship and trust had grown between them. A delighted Tyler invited them to his home where he subtly pumped them for information. The innocent couple were thrilled that this bright young man had such a deep interest in the church; they unadvisedly shared far too much. A short time later, as Laura and Andrew were again witnessing door-to-door, they were picked up by several armed men in a van and brought down to Security Headquarters. While there, the two were put into separate rooms and interrogated for hours. After having been badly beaten, they were transported separately to the county jail for holding. The next day they were taken deep into the country to the National Forest Rehabilitation Center. They were thrown into cells that reeked of fear and death. All around them were humans that looked more like corpses.

"Dear God," Laura prayed, "give us strength in this hour of darkness. Help Andrew and me to shed your light in this dungeon." As Laura's eyes became more accustomed to the dim light, she saw rows of bunk beds with gaunt bodies in most of them. It reminded her of videos she had seen of concentration camps in Nazi Germany, and the grizzly stories she had heard from Jewish residents in the nursing home she and Andrew often visited.

As she settled into one of the few unoccupied bunks, a rough looking lady next to her rasped, "What are you in for?"

As Laura told her that it was for being a Bible-believing Christian, her cellmate asked her, "You're not one of those Adventists are you?"

"Yes, I am!"

"So, your one of those people who are being blamed for all the problems in our country! They say that it's your stubbornness that is causing God to be mad at us! Personally, I'm an agnostic. I could never believe in a God who, just because I *don't* believe in Him, would burn me in a lake of fire forever and ever. And furthermore, I could never serve a God who lets me rot in this hell-hole without any hope of legal intervention to get me out of here. All this just for protesting against the government's overspending. Whatever happened to freedom of speech anyway?"

"That surely does sound unreasonable. But going back to that comment you made about hell. Why do you think that God is going to burn you forever?" asked Laura.

"I grew up in the South—Bill Clanton's little granddaughter Beth—that's me and that's how I know! Every good Southerner knows that if you're not saved, you're going to *that place*. I guess I'm just not predestined to be saved. I'm not really sure there *is* a God. So I figure I might as well join the agnostics."

"My name's Laura Harris. It's good to meet you, Beth. But why do you think you're not predestined to be saved?"

"I don't know exactly. All that religious nonsense is too hard for me to sort out. I mean, if God—who is omni-everything—predestines some to be saved and some to be lost, and you happen to be the *lucky* one that is predestined to be lost, you get to burn in the lake of fire forever and ever. And you have no choice in the matter. What kind of a God would treat His creatures like that? And what about all those who have never heard of Jesus? Are they going to burn forever too? No, thanks, I don't wish to know a God like that; in fact, I hope a God like that *doesn't* exist!"

"Well, I have to admit that I agree with everything you have said thus far."

"YOU WHAT? I thought you said you were a Christian?"

"I did—and I am!" said Laura emphatically, "But I wouldn't serve a God like you have described. The truth is that the Bible doesn't teach predestination or hell in the way many people—and churches—believe."

"This I've got to hear!" says Beth. "If the Bible doesn't teach these things, then what does it teach?"

"The Bible says in John 3:16 that 'God loved the world so much that He gave His one and only son that *whoever* believes in Him won't perish but have everlasting life'. 'Whoever' includes everybody! All have the same chance at eternal life. This, as well as many other Bible texts, tells us that we all have a choice as to whether or not we receive the benefits of Christ's sacrifice—or not. Jesus gave His life that we might have that choice."[1]

"As for burning throughout eternity, that also is not scriptural. As a matter of fact, if the Bible taught that, I'd probably feel the same way you do."[2]

After spending some time discussing God's true character, the two exhausted women decided to get some rest. As Beth drifted off to sleep, new thoughts were awakening in her heart. "I never heard these things before. If they're true, it puts a new slant on the whole deal!"

While the ladies were sharing deep spiritual insights, the Warden was interrogating Andrew in his office, trying to get him to see that it's these stubborn Sabbath keepers that are to blame for all the world's problems.

"I'll give you some time to think about you're seditious ways," said the Warden, "before I send for you again."

The next few days Andrew sat in his lonely cell with plenty of time to think about all that the Warden had said. He remembered reading about this time in the Christian classic 'The Great Controversy'.[3] How each believer would be called to be a true witness for his faith. Andrew prayed for the strength to follow Jesus no matter the cost and a sweet peace came into his soul. That settled it for Andrew. By God's sustaining grace, He would accept the consequences of choosing the right—whatever they might be.[4]

After several more vain attempts to get information out of Andrew that would betray his brethren or to get him to denounce his faith, it was decided that he was worthy of death. Although he had never been officially accused of any crime, he suffered the most inhumane torture. (The U. S. Supreme Court had recently ruled that it was not unconstitutional in times of national emergency for police to use their discretion in the choice of 'aggressive methods of persuasion' in cases of terrorism.) As he was stretched on the rack (that had been brought to the facility from Italy several years after 911) almost beyond the point of human endurance, he was asked again, "Will you turn from this foolishness and promote peace? For the good of mankind and to bring back Gods' blessing on our country, just raise your hand with me and say 'Hail to the Republic of America'?"

"I have nothing to turn from," groaned Andrew between waves of pain. "You haven't shown me from the Bible even one place where I have not been true to God's principles. If I *could* raise my hand," a trickle of blood ran from the corner of John's mouth, his voice a barely audible whisper, so that the Warden had to lean close to hear, "I would pledge to follow my Savior and to keep *all* His commandments."

"Alright then! If you want to remain rebellious and go against the government, then away with you!" declared the infuriated Warden.

Just before Andrew's body succumbed, he softly sang, "My Jesus, I love Thee, I know Thou art mine. For Thee all the folly of sin I resign. My gracious Redeemer, my Savior art Thou. If ever I loved Thee, my Jesus, 'tis now."[5] His last words were a prayer of forgiveness for those who took his life.

A short time later, Laura went through similar treatment in the women's division. She also suffered execution; however, her death was by hanging. As a result of her patient endurance and love, even for her enemies, others with whom she had shared Jesus and who witnessed her death—including Beth—were drawn to the cross. They also received Christ and the wonderful truths that Laura had lived before them. These new believers were also executed. This did not, however, solve the problem for prison officials; instead they discovered, as their predecessors throughout history have also experienced, that the blood of Christian martyrs is seed.

# CHAPTER 13

After several more months of confinement, John was called forth from his cell and escorted to the Warden's office once again. As they made their way through the maze of corridors, John wondered how God had answered his intercessory prayers for the Warden since his last meeting with the prison administrator. His thoughts took a new direction, however, as he became aware that a new man sat behind the large desk.

"Mr. Smith," the new Warden began, "I've been reviewing your file, and I believe we are going to be releasing you soon. Your former boss, Fred Johnson, is no longer CEO of the corporation where you're employed, and it was decided that you would be the best one to take his place. You will be given a home of your choice, wherever you feel is the most advantageous to meet your new responsibilities. Also there will be a full package of executive benefits and a substantial bonus schedule. Congratulations!!" and here the Warden reached across the desk to shake John's hand. "You will never lack for anything. A private jet will also be provided for you and your family—just as the Government's way of saying 'thanks' for your cooperation."

During the Warden's offer, John's flesh was sorely tempted at the prospects of release, worldly security and to see his girls again. He darted a silent prayer to heaven and was spiritually strengthened to resist compromise. "To what 'cooperation' do you refer?" He asked calmly.

"I believe that we have been a little hard on you. Your record indicates that you are an honest man who loves his family, and that you're a diligent worker. And you have your daughters to think about. They really miss you and can't wait to see you. As soon as you are released, you will be flown to where they are." [1]

"Have you harmed my girls?"

"No, not at all! They have been very cooperative, when reasoned with."

"What do you mean? What did you do to them?"

"Oh, don't worry, Mr. Smith; they're fine. All you need to do is sign at the bottom of this document—it's really just a formality—and we will release you, and you can see your girls and go home together."

Carefully John read the letter. It stated that he would desist from all his former activities as an Adventist, give names of the members of his church, where they now met on Sabbaths, and join forces with the ecumenical churches to promote peace and unity within Christendom.

Quietly, but firmly, John said, "I can't sign this!"

The Warden's smile disappeared and his face began to redden. "What do you mean, you can't sign it?" He leaned menacingly across the big desk. "Your life is at stake! Don't you care about your children or our Country?"

"Of course I do! But my first allegiance is to my God and His revealed will. Can light have fellowship with darkness? I cannot sign. I will not!"

In total frustration the Warden screamed, "Away with this traitor to solitary confinement! But before he goes there, help him understand the seriousness of these charges."

John was whipped and severely beaten. He was then thrown into a tiny cubicle almost devoid of light and air. John was about to go into an unconscious state from the loss of blood and lack of oxygen when a bright light filled his cell. At first John thought the cell door had been opened, but as he returned to full consciousness, he realized that a dazzling being in white was supporting him in his arms and gently soothing his wounds. The angel's melodic voice broke the silence: "Hold fast to your faith, John. You are greatly beloved of God. Soon you will see Jesus face-to-face." The Being then disappeared, and John was left in darkness—but with an all-pervading sense of peace and joy.

# CHAPTER 14

As Steven continued with his assignments he had much success in betraying the Adventists.

Before his next assignment, Steven was warned to be very cautious of this next couple. "They have a daughter in the sheriff's department and they are very bewitching," he was told. "Their daughter is not only concerned with their welfare but she is very troubled over this Sunday law as well, of which causes us great concern. If she finds out what we're doing she will warn them. This is why we have put off bringing them in. We don't want her to make any foolish decisions. We would hate to lose a good detective. We especially don't want her father to influence her in the wrong direction".

"Don't worry Sergeant I'll be careful."

"Good because we can't wait any longer," replied the sergeant, "because they are having a damaging effect on what we're trying to accomplish. Their names are Marty and Joy Graybeak and he is, I think around age seventy and she is in her late sixties. They go for walks every morning. They live out in the country. Up until now we have only been concentrating on those in and around the city. But now the time has come for us to branch out and start going after those that live in the country. Marty is a mechanic. So I want you to use the car we give you. Before their walk in the morning we want you to go in the car by their place and break down. We will reverse the spark plugs so it will run rough. You can take it from there."

As Steven's car broke down on the road not far from the Graybeaks' home he saw them come out the front door. He pretended he didn't see them as they came down the road. He'd learned in advance that these two were very sociable, as well as compassionate and would help anyone who needed help. As the Graybeaks approached, he faked a couple of sobs and punched the car. The Graybeaks noticed as they approached him.

"Are you okay?" Joy asked.

"Yes, I guess I'll be okay."

"What seems to be the problem?" inquired Marty.

"My car is running really bad and I don't know what's wrong" responded Steven.

"Do you mind if I take a look at it?" asked Marty.

"I don't mind," said Steven.

"By the way, my name is Marty Graybeak and this is my wife Joy."

"My name is Steven."

"It's nice to make your acquaintance Steven! Does the car run at all? asks Marty.

"Yes, it's just running really rough."

"Well why don't you drive it up to our home and I'll take a look at it after breakfast?"

"I really appreciate your help!"

"We would love to have you stay for breakfast if you're not in too much of a hurry and you haven't eaten yet."

"I'm not in a hurry and it's been a while since I have had a good home cooked meal. I really appreciate your offer. My home was destroyed in that land hurricane and my family we're all killed. So I have been kind of wandering around since then and living out of my car."

"Then I guess that means you don't have a place to live?" Marty inquired sympathetically.

"Well I just stay with friends here and there."

"Don't you have family anywhere?"

"I don't know where they are! With all the disasters and everything else going on we've lost contact."

"What about work?"

"I've just been doing some odd jobs. Nothing stable. I've lost everything."

"Why you poor thing," Joy's voice conveyed pity.

"Steven, I noticed you were sobbing when we first met. Not to pry and all but if it helps to talk about it we're open to listening to you if there's something you wish to discuss."

"Well I guess God is punishing me for all the bad things I've done," pretended Steven.

"Why do you think that?" asked Marty.

"What else could it be? I mean if I was a good person and all, God wouldn't let bad things happen right?"

"If you would allow us, Steven, we would like to share with you from God's Word what He really thinks of all of us. However, let's look under the hood and see what's wrong with your car and get it fixed first. Would that be okay?" offered Marty.

"I guess it won't hurt" said Steven.

After finishing breakfast and fixing the car problem Marty invited Steven into the living room. "If you don't mind I would like to pray before we study Gods Word." After prayer, Marty opened up the Word of God and shared God's plan of redemption for all mankind. He shared with Steven things he had never heard before.

After some time studying Steven exclaimed rather abruptly "I have to go now." He rushed out the door to his car fighting an overwhelming sense of guilt and conviction that he couldn't resist because of all the kindness shown him. "My God," he cried, "if all these things are so then I have been terribly wrong. I have betrayed all these innocent people!" He wept uncontrollably as he continued driving down the road. "Please forgive me!"

He traveled a few more miles before he noticed someone waving him down. When Steven stopped, the stranger rushed around to his window and said urgently, "Tyler you must go back to the Graybeaks home and warn them of their danger."

"How do you know who I am and where I came from?"

"Just go!" commanded the stranger.

Steven put the car in gear and the stranger walked behind the vehicle Steven glanced in his rear view mirror but the stranger was nowhere to be seen. "It must have been an Angel," Steven realized.

He rushed back to the Graybeaks to give his real name, Tyler, and to tell them everything that had just happened. The Graybeaks just sat back and listened in awe. After he told the whole story about his work for the police, Joy spoke to Marty, "Now is the time to leave for the wilderness. Probation is soon to close."

She turned to Tyler, "You will not be safe any longer. Come with us. Soon the Sunday Laws will change to a death decree for Sabbath keepers and the authorities will try to annihilate us. Some are being executed for their faith as we speak but there will soon be a universal death decree for all Sabbath keepers. We must leave before that happens."

"Where will we go?" Tyler asked with surprise.

"We're not sure," Marty said, "but God will direct."

As the three of them left, they traveled only roads that were used by loggers to avoid attention. As the day neared its end, the three were very hungry.

"Let's look for a good place to rest," suggested Joy.

Only moments later, they saw someone up ahead on the side of the road with a fire going and some stew cooking. The stranger welcomed them to share his food. They expressed their thankfulness and gladly joined him. After they finished eating and had rested, the stranger rose, "I must leave now."

A few days later on their journey, again slowed by striking hunger, Tyler noticed an old friend's home up ahead. "Wait here," he said to Marty and Joy. "I know the person who lives up here. Let me go and see if I can get us some food."

"Are you sure that's a good idea?" asked Marty.

"Oh yeah, it will be fine."

Tyler had no way of knowing that since he had left the service of the police, there had been a huge increase in the rewards to anyone who turned over Sabbath keepers. His old friend, however, was well aware of the fact. Bud answered as soon as Tyler knocked on his door.

"Hey Tyler long time no see, how are you doing?"

"I'm great!"

"Come on in. I'll get you a beer."

"Oh thanks but no thanks. I quit drinking."

"To each his own," shrugged Bud.

"Listen Bud, I need your help."

"Sure anything, just name it."

"I'm in need of some food."

"Sure! I'll help in any way I can. Has the economy hit you hard too?"

"Yeah, I guess! Well actually—"

As Tyler shared his new found faith in Jesus Christ, Bud just listened.

After he finished, Bud only responded with, "Very interesting".

Anticipating Bud would have the same excitement that he'd had when he was first convicted of the truth, Tyler wasn't suspicious when Bud excused himself saying, "Let me get some food ready for you".

Bud slipped into another room to make a quick call to the authorities to inform them that there was a terrorist in his home. He had a few questions for the police before giving his address. First, he wanted make sure the reward was enough to solve his own financial needs, and he wanted assurance they would go easy on his friend. A short time later police showed up at his door.

"Bud how could you!" asked Tyler. "You looked so interested in hearing what I had to say."

"I'm sorry man, I hated to do this. It's just that hard times have hit me too, and I really needed the money. They said they'd go easy on you though. I'm sure they just want to question you."

As the sheriff handcuffed Tyler they threw him into the car and brought him down to the Sheriff's Department.

"How could you betray us like this?" the sergeant asked Tyler. "Haven't we been good to you? Haven't we been like your parents? We have given you all that you could ever need. You have done such a good job for us. Have the Graybeaks bewitched you so much that you would forsake the cause of truth? I'm going to let you think about your course for a while." The sergeant listed a few incentives and sent Tyler to be escorted to his own private quarters with lots of food and entertainment. Later in the evening, the sergeant stopped by with a beautiful woman hoping to persuade Tyler to turn from his evil ways.

"Tyler, we want to reward you for all your hard work. Perhaps we haven't done everything that we could have done. You're young, and there's a lot you should consider for your future. There's much to be gained from putting aside the confusing ideas the Graybeaks gave you. Consider it."

All it would take was one slip, and Tyler would be back on track. The sergeant left, confident that young woman would be able to slip past Tyler's defenses and reverse the Graybeaks' brainwashing.

The young woman began to try to persuade him. As Tyler struggled with the temptation he wondered if he can resist. He remembers the story of Joseph from Sunday School when he was met with the same fierce temptations, but wondered if he could find the same power to resist as Joseph did. He knew the devil would use anything to lead him away from the truth. *Dear God* Tyler prayed, *after all I've done I don't know if you can hear me or strengthen me in this hour of need, but if you can, please help me right now to resist this temptation.*

# CHAPTER 15

Meanwhile, the Graybeaks were being hunted by K-9 units without success. The angels had guided their footsteps, leading them along the way. In the wilderness they prayed earnestly that Tyler would be protected and that he would stay faithful till the end, whatever the cost.

"Look Marty, up ahead! It looks like a family." They drew closer and noticed the family was singing 'Lift up the trumpet'. "That's music to my ears," Joy said to Marty.

"Mommy, Daddy, look, there's some people coming."

"Please join us, won't you?" the children's father to the Graybeaks.

"We would love to join you. We noticed you were singing 'Lift Up the Trumpet.' Are you Sabbath keepers?"

"Yes we are!"

"We could tell from your demeanor and by the way you were singing," said Joy.

"Praise God we are too!" said Marty.

"Amazing! Truly amazing. By the way, I'm Marty, and this is my wife Joy."

"It's nice to meet both of you. I'm Paul and this is my wife Val, and these are our kids Sonny and Jasmine."

"Where are you from?" asked Marty.

"We're from Fort Smith."

"You've walked a long way," said Marty. "How long have you been traveling?"

"We left our home about five weeks ago. It was only by God's grace that we got out when we did. Our older daughter Tiffany turned us over to the authorities. But we got out of the area before they could find us."

"Praise God that you got out," replied Joy. "I'm sorry that your daughter turned you in. We need to pray for her. As long as Jesus is still interceding on our behalf, there is still hope."

"Amen!" cries Val with tears in her eyes. "We are continually praying."

"Do you have kids?" Paul asked Marty.

"Yes, we have four between the two of us."

"Are they grown up?"

"Yes, all but two live in other states."

"Are they believers?"

"Most of them have chosen their careers and lifestyles above God," Marty said sadly.

"Sorry to hear that." Paul placed his hand on Marty's shoulder.

"But we still hope and believe they will turn to God before probation closes," added Joy.

Curious, Joy continued, "What have you eaten for the last several weeks?"

"Well mostly we have been eating berries and herbs along the way. Other times during our journey we've come across a stranger with a little campfire with stew and sweet bread. He's invited us to join him."

"Did he have enough for all of you?"

"Well… yes! Now that you mention it, he never ran out till we all had our fill. The pot wasn't large enough to feed us all. Why, how did—?"

"Mommy, did Jesus feed us?"

"Why, it must have been an angel."

"Mom it happened when we were at our weakest point and we couldn't find any berries or herbs."

"Now that you mention it" said Paul, "'the Spirit of Prophecy' does say that when we are on the run God will provide, right up until the time that Jesus returns in the clouds.[1] Praise God! He is so good."

"The same thing happened to us!" Joy smiled. "We never need to worry. 'If he cares for the birds of the air and feeds them how much more does He care for us.'[2] God also promises that 'never will I leave you; never will I forsake you.'"[3]

"Paul, how did you come to know about the message?" asks Marty.

"It wasn't very long ago when I preached against the Adventists. I told my congregation that these people were Judaizers, and that they earned salvation by works."

"So you were a preacher then?"

"That's right Marty, I was a Pentecostal minister. I had the largest church in my area. I believed in telling it like it was, straight from the pulpit. Or at least I preached what I believed was the straight message. There were some doctrines that the church believed that I just could never be settled with."

"Did anyone know this?"

"Just my wife. She also saw things that she wasn't satisfied with. But what do you do? I was a minister. I was a preacher of righteousness. I couldn't tell anyone that I was feeling this way. So I went on for years like this. Then one day I got a book in the mail. It was talking about this National Sunday law that was going to come. I threw it down the first time. Then a short time later I was at a grocery store and I saw another one in the shopping cart. I started getting curious but again I resisted taking it. Then the next Sunday a parishioner came to me and told me that a worker read this book and was convinced it was the truth. She asked me to read it to see if I could find any errors in it."

"Was it the same book every time?" asked Marty.

"Yes! So of course, I had a good reason to read it. I mean after all I had to protect my members from false doctrines. But secretly I was wondering if just maybe God was trying to speak to me. I tried to shrug away that idea. I told my church member that I would get back with her. I read it through quickly the first time sure that I would be able to detect any error right off. But I hadn't detected anything wrong and I was determined to find some problem. After all, it went against everything I believed in and had been teaching all these years."

"So did you find anything wrong with the book?" asked Joy.

"No but as I studied the book further I started becoming angry. More than once I threw the book down disgusted. Pride just wouldn't let go. I was determined to get to the bottom of this whole thing once and for all. One night I stayed up all night long studying. At one point I broke down and cried uncontrollably. I started to realize that maybe I had been duped. All these years at the height of my profession, I realized that I knew nothing.

"For the first time in my life all the pieces of the puzzle fit together perfectly. I accepted the Sabbath, state of the dead, all of it.

After that, I had perfect peace, Marty. It was a peace that I had never before experienced. I knew the truth and the truth had set me free!"[4]

"So what happened at your church after that?" asked Joy.

"As I said, I had perfect peace when I discovered this wonderful message, but that was about to change. You see I was so excited about this new found truth that I was certain that my parishioners would be eager to accept it."

"What was their response?"

"The next Sunday, the sermon started out fine, but halfway into the message regarding the Sabbath, people started getting restless. There was an outburst. It started with one of the elders. Up out of his seat, he charged at me like a ferocious animal dashing towards its victim. Other people started screaming and dashing into the aisles and running towards me. They ran up on the platform ready to tear me apart. Then all of a sudden, they all stopped, went, and sat down."

"You've got to be joking!" Joy blurted out.

"No! The only thing I could guess as to what happened was that God intervened and took control of the situation. I was able to finish my message. Only a few responded to my appeal and came forward. I thought my congregation would have been eager to give themselves fully to God. They always appeared to be open to the things of God. They were joyful and excited in the Lord, singing, speaking in tongues, and praising God in church. Boy was I in for an awakening. Those who stood closest to me for years were the first to tear me apart. I couldn't believe what was happening. If someone told me beforehand what was about to take place, I never would have believed them. Don't get me wrong there are many beautiful believers in the denomination, but I was so saddened that the members of my church responded this way."

"So what happened then? Did you ever join a Sabbath keeping church?"

"To tell you the truth, I had no interest in leaving my church. I just assumed that I could bring everything back together again and settle things. I remembered how I felt after I was exposed to this truth and thought that in time these members that were against me at first just didn't understand what I was saying. I comforted myself with the feeling that after I spent time with them explaining from the scriptures 'whether these things were so'[5] that they would see the importance of the Sabbath.

"Unbeknownst to me, the few that raised a commotion started calling members and getting a petition to have me removed as a Pentecostal Minister."

"The next thing I knew I received a call from headquarters asking to meet to discuss some concerns that they had. We set up a time at the church for a few days later. To my surprise the church was packed. I started getting nervous. Then before I went inside I prayed not only for wisdom but for discernment and protection as well. As I proceeded to the front of the church I saw some of the other leaders from my church looking at me with an 'I'll show you who's in control' sort of attitude. When I reached the front I saw the main conference leaders sitting on the front pew. The long and short of it all was that the meeting that we were supposed to have ended up being a witch-hunt. I had never been treated so unfairly in my life."

"They gave you a chance to explain your position didn't they?" asked Joy with hope.

"I wasn't given an opportunity to explain my position at all. Every time I tried, I was interrupted. All I was given the opportunity to do was to say whether or not I still held to certain tenets of the faith of the denomination and whether or not I accepted Sunday as the Christian Sabbath and that Christ had changed the day of worship after His resurrection. 'But this is not true,' I kept trying to say. 'Nowhere in Scripture are these changes mentioned. The Catholic Church made these changes. They, along with other churches even admit to it.'[6] All my reasoning fell on deaf ears. I was disfellowshipped and I lost everything including my pension."

Joy was surprised, "Your pension? I never knew they could do that."

"Yes, I guess since the terrorist and hate laws passed eventually they included anyone who preached hate against any other churches."

"But you weren't preaching hate."

"I know that and you know that, but if the state suspects that you have evil intent, they've got you."

"Do you mean to tell me that even a couple years ago before the Sunday law took effect that they were using the hate crime bills against Christians?"

"I'm afraid so, Joy."

"Wow, then what did you do? Could you collect unemployment?"

"Well no! The unemployment office said I had no right to benefits. I lost my home, my daughter and everything I owned. That is except for my beautiful wife and other two lovely children."

"Don't forget Jesus too, Daddy."

"That's right honey, especially Jesus."

"That's an amazing story," responded Marty. "What did you do after that?"

"It gets a little complicated after that Marty. I'll give you the short version for now. I got a job that paid a little better than minimum wage for a while, and my wife found work too."

"Did you ever join the Sabbath keeping church?"

"I really didn't have that much interest in the idea at first. Mostly because of preconceived ideas that were out there. Then, after a while of continuing my study of God's word, I realized that these Sabbath keepers weren't as far off as I first thought. I wanted to learn more but I guess you could say I was a little apprehensive. I knew they were having a camp-meeting in town so I decided to go hear some of the speakers. I was really moved by the messages and wanted to talk to someone when I had something happen that changed my mind."

"You did! What was that?"

"You see Marty, on Sabbath morning there were some people passing out brochures. I met one. His name was Fred Araback. He was very pleasant and mild mannered. I assumed he was with this group. That is until I read his magazine. It taught that probation had closed for the church, and now God was calling His people out of Babylon including the churches. As you can imagine, this was confusing. Many of the pioneers' writings of this church and Ellen White were quoted to justify this teaching."[7]

"So then what did you do?"

"I decided to dig deeper. I went online to the Ellen White Estates in Michigan and started reading all the material that I could read on these subjects. I discovered that the pioneer writings were grossly misquoted, and much of what they actually said on the given subjects were not used.

"I received material from others on the feast days. These brochures said that they were still binding on us as Christians today.

There again, very little support to justify these claims. I don't know why they even used Ellen White to justify their teachings when she didn't endorse these teachings at all."

"Did all these 'winds of doctrine' turn you off from Sabbath keeping churches?" asked Marty.

"Well to be honest," chuckled Paul, "I actually wrote a rebuttal against them. I wasn't even a part of this church. Why was I defending them? But it pushed me, and I really wanted to learn more. I started watching, a Sabbath keeping television network, and I started attending a local Sabbath church as well. I introduced myself to the pastor of the church. He recognized me from the radio program that I used to have before I was disfellowshipped from the Pentecostal church. After I shared my experience with Pastor Alfred J Mackson, he was excited and asked if I would like to study further. I agreed and after much study I decided, along with my wife and two kids, to unite with Sabbath keepers.

"Did you have any difficulty with any other doctrines?" asked Joy.

"Some things didn't come easy. The subject that I found most disagreeable was the subject on tongues. But I soon realized that the gifts of the Spirit were for the express purpose of building up the Church, not oneself.[8]

"I also had a hard time understanding the Sanctuary Message. Afterward, though, I realized that the message of the sanctuary is the one pillar that holds all the other teachings of the Adventist church together. I could see later that the devil didn't want me to understand this message for that reason.[9] When I sorted through all these things I was ready to join the Adventist church. I have been learning much these last few years since becoming an Adventist. Since the Sunday law has been advancing in stages I believe His coming is at the door."

"Praise God! Thank you for that great testimony brother."

"Listen," Joy whispered urgently, "I thought I heard something! It sounds like a helicopter!"

Paul spoke quietly. "Keep low. Don't make any noises."

"They're flying really low," whispered Marty. "Oh no, they're landing over there in that opening. We have to run."

"Wait!" urged Val. "We must pray."

They all got down on their knees together and asked God for strength and protection.

Voices and footsteps grew nearer. An authoritative voice, presumably the captain, called to another group of men, "The heat sensor shows them to be over there."

Heavily armed men with eyes filled with vengeance surrounded the two families who remained in an attitude of prayer.

The captain spoke. "Fire." Marty, Joy, and the others' ears rang as loud shots fired from every weapon, but not one of the trapped civilians fell to the ground.

The captain's voice sounded again. "What's the matter with you men? How could you miss point blank shots? For real this time. Fire!" Shots flew through the air in every direction but hit no one.

"What in the world is going on?" the captain screamed.

"The guns aren't working right, Captain," one of the men replied frantically.

"Fine, just tear them into pieces." The men dropped their guns and rushed the Adventists, but were each frozen in place by an unseen force.

"I said to attack them!" shouted the frustrated captain, but the soldiers couldn't move.

"Look!" Sonny pointed out to his family and their new friends. "The soldiers can't move. See the men with shining swords raising their hands? No one can go past them!"

"If you imbeciles can't follow a command then I will do it myself." The captain raised his gun, but the wind began to whip around him and the earth opened without explanation, swallowing him where he stood.

In terror, most of the soldiers ran away, while perfect peace surrounded the saints. Some of the men cried out, "This is the hand of God!"

Just beyond the treeline, two of the soldiers collapsed, gasping for breath. "Could we have been wrong about these Sabbath keepers?" one asked. "We burned their churches down and killed many of them."

The other shook his head, "The 'Being' we saw and heard everywhere told us the Sabbath was changed from Saturday to Sunday.

He said he was the Christ. He told us to rid the earth of these troublers of Israel."

In the silence, as the two caught their breath, the first man repeated, "Could we have been wrong?"

In the time that followed, these two man and others like them approached the Sabbath keepers, crying out, "Show us how we can be saved from God's wrath." But as they begged for words from God's people, they discovered everything had been said already. Every opportunity had been given to each person, but so many had chosen to follow man and tradition above the true Word of God.

# Chapter 16

"Mr. Smith, come with me." A guard escorted John back to the warden's office.

"Have a seat," the warden offered. Moments later the guards entered with a man who was badly beaten.

"Pastor Sven, what have they done to you?" John gasped.

"Do you know this man?" the warden asked.

"Of course I do. He's my pastor. What have you done to him?"

"Mr. Smith, you both have committed very serious crimes against humanity. Are you going to listen to reason?"

"If you are asking me to retract my convictions, I still cannot."

The warden backhanded the pastor and ordered, "Guards, show Mr. Smith what we do to terrorists who disobey our orders. If Mr. Smith has any sympathy for his pastor then he'll reason with us."

As the guards beat Pastor Sven, John's heart ached and he begged them, "No, please stop."

"John," whispered the pastor in faint gasps, "do not give up your faith no matter what they may do. Jesus will come – soon! Forever!"

"You're living a fantasy!" the warden shouted in frustration.

"I love you, Pastor." John began to weep. "Oh, Lord. Please forgive these men their sins against You. Strengthen us and my children and all your faithful ones in this hour of trial. Amen!"

The warden answered his ringing phone. "Warden," said the voice on the other end of the line, "a mandate was just issued to execute all remaining Sabbath keepers at a predetermined time. Details will be faxed momentarily."

With these two men suddenly no longer an issue, the warden calmly ordered the guards to put them both in confinement near the execution chamber.

"John," the pastor whispered, "remember the promise that 'He who is faithful to death will receive the crown of life'."[1]

"Thank you, friend."

The guards escorted the men toward their cells. From every side, the words rang out even from the other prisoners: "Rid the earth of them!" They turned a corner into another corridor where inmates were supposed to be lining up for recreational time. Most rushed like wild animals toward Pastor Sven and John. Their attack failed when they were stopped in their tracks by an unseen hand, and the two men were delivered safely to their cells.

Simultaneously, all around the earth, the order was given to execute all Sabbath keepers at the earliest opportunity.

A helicopter landed near Fred and Jackie's cabin. Heavily armed men stormed the building with orders not to come back until all occupants were executed.

Fred had spotted the helicopter before it landed and had alerted everyone to run. It was a chase, and a long exhausting one.

The military radioed to neighboring areas to be on the lookout for Fred and his family. Not only the military but even former Sabbath keepers, citizens from the surrounding community searched the area. Finally someone radioed the others, "We have them. All five of them." Everyone in range rushed to attack the believers. Fred and the others were amazed as men in shining garments surrounded them with flaming swords. The oppressors froze in their tracks, paralyzed, and they remained this way, awaiting the tempests that would shake them free, only moments away.

At around the same time, Sabbath keepers being held as prisoners all over the country and around the world were brought out to the gallows, lined up before firing squads, and pushed before chopping blocks. As ropes were grabbed, triggers half-pulled, and axes mid-air, nature gave way. Thunder crashed, lightning cracked, and an earthquake trembled as never before. Sabbath-keeping "terrorists" forgotten, the would-be executors abandoned their posts, trying to escape the crumbling mountains and car-sized hail.

In the space of a moment, a bright light shone from every direction and angels appeared above, fanning out, multiplying until the sky was filled with them.

As the world beheld the glory in the sky, nonbelievers had flashbacks of how they had treated God's children. Some fell to their knees. Other tried to place blame, turning on one another and targeting their superiors. "You told us to persecute these people!" Religious leaders overseeing the executions were particular targets. "You led us to Sunday worship, to shun the Sabbath. You are responsible!"

Oceans and seas broke into a unified tempest, terrorizing the unbelievers as they realized even further the power of the true and living God they had denied. The deceived and the deceivers rushed at one another. Finally, Satan gained full control of the world as the Spirit of God withdrew and every previous restraint was removed.

Amid the angels above, the Son of God appeared in plain sight of all and nature fell silent as quickly as it had erupted. "Jesus!" cried each one who had awaited this moment. Hundreds, thousands of believers around the world recognized their Savior, with tears of gladness and fulfillment.

The focus of eternity rested on God's people as their chains and shackles fell to the ground. Each person, each family looked upon the Son of God and spoke not from Scripture memorized, but from the deepest part of their souls, from relief and joy. "Surely this is our God; we have trusted in Him and He saved us." Graves of all the redeemed opened up, and the dead were given life again. They began to rise, not just from their resting places, but into the air where the living faithful were caught up with them also. They moved on and upward, away from the evil earth, to meet the Lord in the air. Everywhere, families were reunited and cries of joy were heard.

# Chapter 17

John and Pastor Sven had been escorted into the execution chamber, but now found themselves free as the prison building had crumbled around them. The saw all the glory of the Son of God and had exclaimed praise with all the other believers around the world.

"John!" cried a voice behind him.

He turned, "Lisa!" They ran to each other's arms.

Music to his ears, little voices called out, "Mommy! Daddy!"

The family reunited, they held each other kissing cheeks and foreheads, crying with joy. "My babies!"

John clung to all of them. "Oh, how we missed you, Lisa. Now we get to be together and with Jesus through all eternity."

"Fred, Jackie, Tara, yes and, over there, is that Tyler? Let's go see! Why it is Tyler also. Praise God! Let"s look for our other kids. I hope I get to hold them in my arms again."

There were more voices. " John and Lisa! We have you to thank for sharing these truths with us. We accepted it sometime before probation closed and the plagues were poured out."

John turned again and exclaimed, "Why, it's even the warden who had me in his office the first time."

The warden declared, "John, your testimony was so powerful that I could not refute it. I tried having you released but there was no way. As soon as I accepted the truth, I was removed from my office and shot in the courtyard.[1] I didn't even have time to see if my family believed my testimony before I was killed. I must see if I can find them. I am so grateful I made the right decision."

"Me too," said John. He turned to Lisa. "Look over there. It's Pastor Sven. Thank you for helping us in our walk of faith. While many pastors caved in under the pressure, you stood fast and were faithful."

"Preparation in the simple times made it easier to stand for the truth in hard times John. We have eternity with Jesus as the culmination of those truths," responded Pastor Sven.

"And, could it be? Why it's Debbie and Michelle. I am so excited," responded John.

"We're happy to be here John," responded Debbie.

"Thank you for your families witness. That had much to do with me coming to Jesus before it was too late."

"It was our privilege Michelle. We never gave up praying for you."

After more families were reunited they were escorted toward Heaven by angels.[2]

"Look Daddy and Mommy," said Tara, "There's the man who was by the side of the road, and who gave us that vehicle."

Fred declared, "So you were my angel!"

"Yes, I was with you every step of the way. I helped you take all the right turns when you were going into and out of the city, in spite of most of the roads being blocked," explained the angel. "I was protecting you when you didn't even know you were in danger."

"And here's the angel who supported me while I was in prison," said John.

"I was there all the way for you John. Not just in prison. But every time you witnessed for our Creator, I protected you from being stoned or shot at or beaten to death. I delivered you many times."

"Thank you," said John.

The angel bowed his head and spoke. "Thanks all belong to our Creator, the one who gave His life for the human race. When He was being beaten and His beard plucked out, and He was spit upon, all the powers of Hell were let loose. All the angels were ready for Him to just give the word, and we would have silenced His enemies in a moment. They said to Him, "If you are the Christ, the Son of the Living God, then free yourself from that cross." We were just waiting for the word to be spoken. But instead of being delivered from this world He said 'Father forgive them for they know not what they do'"[3].

"It's amazing He did all that for me," John said.

"Yes John. We couldn't understand how He could subject Himself to the death of the cross. But now we see it was to save the human race.

"Now, with everything made clear, I think of that time so long ago when the former head angel, Lucifer, now Satan, tried to turn us away from God, accusing Him of being controlling and vindictive, many angels believed him. As a result they were kicked out of heaven down to this earth. After Adam and Eve fell for the lies, the controversy started all over again on this earth. Up until the time of the death of Christ, there was still a question in many of the angels' minds, along with the on-looking universe and unfallen worlds as to whether or not Satan was justified in any of his claims or his actions. Evil's true colors were seen after Satan put Christ to death on the cross by using the religious leaders of His day.

"Later in Earth's history, during the Dark Ages, Satan gained control of the church again and put to death millions more Christians. Many were martyred because they were Sabbath-keepers, just like those you've witnessed, John."

"The controversy through the ages has revolved around worship. God memorialized the seventh day at creation to show that He created everything. He reminded people throughout the ages that He had set apart the seventh day. His law even declared His people should observe the Sabbath day. But Satan came and deceived many by turning them away from the day that God sanctified, hallowed and blessed. Instead, he created a substitute sabbath, which was Sunday. So you see John, the struggle between Sabbath and Sunday isn't just over a day. It's about who was going to receive your allegiance, Christ or Satan. Because you chose Christ, I was assigned to you for your earthly life. I was so happy when you accepted Pastor Sven's invitation that day to surrender your all to God and His service. Everyone that chose Christ as their Lord and Savior was assigned an angel."

The angel pointed to a group of people not far away who were greeting one another with joy. "Those that you see right over there witnessed with their lives because of their pastor who turned them over to the authorities."

"Really" responded John. "Who are they?"

"When persecution came and Satan appeared, he bewitched many, and they crumbled under the pressure. This was the scenario with many pastors and church members who turned on the faithful and handed them over to be martyred. There were many people who professed to know Jesus, but acted on Satan's temptations instead, showing by their works who they had really accepted. Some pretended at faithfulness but when others weren't around, they lived a different lifestyle. As you know, not everyone chose Christ in the end.

"You will have the next 1,000 years to review all the stories of all the lives you wish to examine. You'll also have the opportunity to understand why you aren't seeing Bob and some of the other people you expected to see. But God's judgment is gracious and fair. Everyone will have the chance to understand it."

"I really want to talk to some of the people whose faithful ways cost them their lives. But first, I want to meet the one who gave His life for me, who bore with me through thick and thin." John smiled broadly. "Can we go meet Jesus now?"

Joy, Marty, Tyler, and so many more found their way to one another and made their way to kneel at the feet of Jesus. This was Heaven, and Heaven was worth it all.

# APPENDIX

Bible quotations are from the New International Version (NIV) unless otherwise stated, or unless it is quoted from other sources.

**Chapter 1**
1. Psalms 91:1, 2, 4, 7

**Chapter 3**
1. Verduin, Leonard, Reformers and their Stepchildren (Grand Rapids: Eerdmans, 1964), 292.
2. Daniel 3

**Chapter 5**
1. Exodus 20: 13; Gen. 19; Gen 6:5, 6, 7, 11, 12; Romans 1:24–32

**Chapter 6**
1. Ephesians 4: 31-32
2. Romans 1
3. http://www.barna.org/FlexPage.aspx?Page=BarnaupdateandBarnaUpdateID=106.
4. John 14:16, 17; Matthew 12:35 -37; Revelation 14:7; Hebrews 9:27; Romans 1: 28-88 32.
5. Bible proof texts for this subject can be found in Romans 6:23; 2 Thessalonians 2:8; Ecclesiastes 9:5, 6; Job 14: 12–14, 21; 1 Corinthians 15: 20–22, 51–55; Psalms 146:4; John 11:11-14, 24; 6:40; 1 Thessalonians 4:13–16; Genesis 3:19; Acts 17:30-31; 1 Corinthians 4:5; Isaiah 26:19-21; Revelation 20: 10, 12-15; 21:8; Ezekiel 28: 18, 19; Jude 7; Malachi 4:1. Texts are taken from : Vining, Noble B., Bible Textionary, (Chattanooga: 1984). For this and any other Bible studies mentioned in this book go online to www.bibleuniverse.com.

**Chapter 7**
1. John 10:10.
2. Genesis 2:15-17.
3. Genesis 3:4.

4. White, E.G, Manuscript Release, Vol. 6, 1892.
5. White, E.G., Review and Herald, June 4, 1901.
6. Genesis 4:8
7. White, E.G., Review and Herald, April 29, 1875
8. White, E.G., Review and Herald, March 2, 1901
9. White, E.G., Review and Herald, June 4, 1901

## Chapter 8

1. For a deeper study on this topic see these Bible texts: Genesis 2:2, 3; Exodus 16:4,5; 14-36; 20: 8-11; 31: 12-18; Deuteronomy 5: 12-15; Matthew 5: 16-20; Mark 1: 21;6:2; Luke 13: 11-17; Acts 13: 14; 18:4; 13:42-44; 16:13; Revelation 1:10; Exodus 20:10; Leviticus 23:1-3; Mark 2:28; Genesis 1: 5-31; Leviticus 23:32; Mark 1: 21,32; Exodus 16: 23; 31: 13-17; Isaiah 56: 1-7; Hebrews 4: 1-11; Isaiah 58: 13,14; Ezekiel 20:12,20; Matthew 12: 12; 24: 20; Mark 2: 27,28; Isaiah 66:23. These texts are taken from The Bible Textionary

2. Exodus 20: 8-11.
3. Ezekiel 20:12, 20; Rev. 22:14; Is.66:23; John 14:15; John 15:10.
4. White, E.G., Review and Herald April 23, 1901

## Chapter 9

1. "Those who honor the Bible Sabbath will be denounced as enemies of law and order, as breaking down the moral restraints of society, causing anarchy and corruption, and calling down the judgments of God upon the earth. Their conscientious scruples will be pronounced obstinacy, stubbornness, and contempt of authority. They will be accused of disaffection toward the government. Ministers who deny the obligation of the divine law will present from the pulpit the duty of yielding obedience to the civil authorities as ordained of God. In legislative halls and courts of justice, commandment keepers will be misrepresented and condemned. A false coloring will be given to their words; the worst construction will be put upon their motives. As the Protestant churches reject the clear, Scriptural arguments in defense of Gods law, they will long to silence those whose faith they cannot overthrow by the Bible. Though they blind their eyes to the fact, they are

now adopting a course which will lead to the persecution of those who conscientiously refuse to do what the rest of the Christian world are doing, and acknowledge the claims of the papal Sabbath. The dignitaries of church and state will unite to bribe, persuade, or compel all classes to honor the Sunday. The lack of divine authority will be supplied by oppressive enactments. Political corruption is destroying love of justice and regard for truth; and even in free America, rulers and legislators, in order to secure public favor, will yield to the popular demand for a law enforcing Sunday observance. Liberty of conscience, which has cost so great a sacrifice, will no longer be respected. In the soon-coming conflict we shall see exemplified the Prophets words: 'The dragon was wroth with the woman, and went to make war with the remnant of her seed, which keep the commandments of God, and have the testimony of Jesus Christ. White, E.G. Great Controversy, (Mountain View: Pacific Press Pub. Assoc., 1911) 592

    2. Mark Sidwell, ed. Scenes from American Church History (Greenville: Bob Jones Univ. Press, 1991),1, 2

    3. "Among the Christian exiles who first fled to America and sought an asylum from royal oppression and priestly intolerance were many who determined to establish a government upon the broad foundation of civil and religious liberty. Their views found place in the Declaration of Independence, which sets forth the great truth that 'all men are created equal' and endowed with the inalienable right to 'life, liberty, and the pursuit of happiness.' And the constitution guarantees to the people the right of self-government, providing that representatives elected by the popular vote shall enact and administer the laws. Freedom of religion was also granted, every man being permitted to Worship God according to the dictates of his conscience. Republicanism and Protestantism became the fundamental principles of the nation. These principles are the secret of its power and prosperity. The oppressed and downtrodden throughout Christendom have turned to this land with interest and hope. Millions have sought its shores, and the United States has risen to a place among the most powerful nations of the earth. But the beast with lamblike horns 'spake as a dragon. And he exerciseth all the power of the first beast before him, and causeth the earth and them which dwell therein to worship the first beast, whose deadly wound was healed;... saying to them that dwell on the earth, that they should make

an image to the beast, which had the wound by the sword, and did live.' Revelation 13:11-14. The lamblike horns and dragon voice of the symbol point to a striking contradiction between the professions and the practice of the nation thus represented. The 'speaking' of the nation is the action of its legislative and judicial authorities. By such action it will give the lie to those liberal and peaceful principles which it has put forth as the foundation of its policy. The prediction that it will speak 'as a dragon' and exerciseth 'all the power of the first beast' plainly foretells a development of the spirit of intolerance and persecution that was manifested by the nations represented by the dragon and the leopardlike beast. And the statement that the beast with two horns 'causeth the earth and them which dwell therein to worship the first beast' indicates that the authority of this nation is to be exercised in enforcing some observance which shall be an act of homage to the papacy. Such action would be directly contrary to the principles of this government, to the genius of its free institutions, to the direct and solemn avowals of the Declaration of Independence, and to the Constitution. The founders of the nation wisely sought to guard against the employment of secular power on the part of the church, with its inevitable result- intolerance and persecution. The Constitution provides that 'Congress shall make no law respecting an establishment of religion, or prohibiting the free exercise thereof,' and that 'no religious test shall ever be required as a qualification of any office of public trust under the United States.' Only in flagrant violation of these safeguards to the nation's liberty, can any religious observance be enforced by civil authority. But the inconsistency of such action is no greater than is represented in the symbol. It is the beast with lamblike horns- in profession pure, gentle, and harmless-that speaks as a dragon. 'Saying to them that dwell on the earth, that they should make an image to the beast.' .... When the early church became corrupted by departing from the simplicity of the gospel and accepting heathen rites and customs, she lost the Spirit and power of God; and in order to control the consciences of the people, she sought the support of the secular power. The result was the papacy, a church that controlled the power of the state and employed it to further her own ends. Whenever the church has obtained secular power, she has employed it to punish dissent from her doctrines. Protestant churches that have followed in the steps of Rome by forming alliance with worldly powers have manifested similar desire to restrict liberty of conscience. An example of this is given in the long-continued persecution of dissenters by the Church of England. During the sixteenth and seventeenth centuries, thousands of nonconformist ministers were forced to flee from their churches, and many, both of pastors and people, were subjected to fine, imprisonment, torture, and martyrdom. It was apostasy that led the early church to seek the aid of the civil government, and this prepared the way for the development of the papacy-the beast. Said Paul: 'There' shall 'come a falling away . . . and that man of sin be revealed.' 2 Thess. 2:3. So apostasy in the church will prepare the way for the image to the beast. The Bible declares that before the coming of the Lord there will exist a state of religious declension similar to that in the first centuries. 'In the last days perilous times shall come. For men shall be lovers of their own selves, covetous, boasters, proud, blasphemers, disobedient to parents, unthankful, unholy, without natural affection, trucebreakers, false accusers, incontinent, fierce, despisers of those that are good, traitors, heady, high minded, lovers of pleasure more than lovers of God; having a form of godliness, but denying the power thereof' 2 Tim. 3: 1-5. Now the Spirit speaketh expressly, that in the latter times some shall depart from the faith, giving heed to seducing spirits, and doctrines of devils.' 1 Tim. 4:1. Satan will work 'with all power and signs and lying wonders, and with all deceivableness of unrighteousness.' And all that received not the love of the truth, that they might be saved,' will be left to accept strong delusion, that they should believe a lie.' 2 Thess. 2: 9-11. When this state of ungodliness shall be reached, the same results will follow as in the first centuries.... When the leading churches of the United States, uniting upon such points of doctrine as are held by them in common, shall influence the state to enforce their decrees and to sustain their institutions, then Protestant America will have formed an image of the Roman hierarchy, and the infliction of civil penalties upon dissenters will inevitably result. The beast with two horns 'causeth [commands] all, both small and great, rich and poor, free and bond, to receive a mark in their right hand, or in their foreheads: and that no man might buy or sell, save he that had the mark, or the name of the beast, or the number of his name.' Rev. 13:16, 17. The third angels warning is: 'If any man worship the beast and his image, and receive his mark in his forehead, or in his hand, the same shall drink of the wine of the wrath of God.' 'The beast' mentioned in this message, whose worship is enforced by the two horned beast, is the first, or leopardlike beast of Rev. 13- the papacy. The 'image to the beast' represents that form of apostate Protestantism which will be developed when the Protestant churches shall seek the aid of the civil power for the enforcement of their dogmas. ... since those who keep Gods commandments and thus placed in contrast with those that worship the beast and his image and receive his mark, it follows that the keeping of Gods law, on the one hand, and its violation, on the other, will make the distinction between the worshippers of God and the worshippers of the beast. The special characteristic of the beast, and therefore of his image, is the breaking of Gods commandments. Says Daniel, of the little horn, the papacy: 'He shall think to change times and the law.' Dan. 7:25, R.V. and Paul styled the same power the 'man of sin,' who was to exalt himself above God. One prophecy is a complement of the other. Only by changing Gods law could the papacy exalt itself above God; whoever should understandingly keep the law as thus changed would be giving supreme honor to that power by which the change was made. Such an act of obedience to papal laws would be a mark of allegiance to the pope in the place of God. The papacy has attempted to change the law of God. The second commandment, forbidding image worship, has been dropped from the law, and the fourth commandment, has been so changed as to authorize the observance of the first instead of the seventh day as the Sabbath. But papists urge, as a reason for omitting the second commandment, that it is unnecessary, being included in the first, and that they are giving the law exactly as God designed it to be understood. This cannot be the change foretold by the prophet. An intentional, deliberate change is presented: He shall think to change the times and the law.' The change in the fourth commandment exactly fulfills the prophecy. For this the only authority claimed is that of the church. Here the papal power openly sets itself above God. While the worshippers of God will be especially distinguished by their regard for the fourth commandment,- since this is the sign of His creative power and the witness to His claim upon mans reverence and homage,- the worshippers of the beast will be distinguished by their efforts to tear down the Creators memorial, to exalt the institution of Rome." White, Great Controversy, 441–446.

    4. Rev. 18:2–4; 8–21; 13:16,17; 15:2; 16:2; 14:10,11; Mal.4:1–3.
    5. Rev. 14: 9-11; 13: 1-15; 13:8,18.

6. Exodus 20:8-11; Ezek. 20:12,20.

**Chapter 10**
1. Psalms 91; 37:25.
2. Isaiah 58: 12, 13.

**Chapter 11**
1. "Heretofore those who presented the truths of the third angel's message have often been regarded as mere alarmists. Their predictions that religious intolerance would gain control in the United States, that church and state would unite to persecute those who keep the commandments of God, have been pronounced groundless and absurd. It has been confidently declared that this land could never become other than what it has been- the defender of religious freedom. But as the question of enforcing Sunday observance is widely agitated, the event so long doubted and disbelieved is seen to be approaching, and the third message will produce an effect which it could not have had before.... As the people go to their former teachers with the eager inquiry, Are these things so? The ministers will present fables, prophesy smooth things, to soothe their fears and quiet the awakened conscience. But since many refused to be satisfied with the mere authority of men and demand a plain "Thus saith the Lord," the popular ministry, like the Pharisees of old, filled with anger as their authority is questioned, will denounce the message as of Satan and stir up the sin-loving multitudes to revile and persecute those who proclaim it. As the controversy extends into new fields and the minds of the people are called to Gods downtrodden law, Satan is astir. The power attending the message will only madden those who oppose it. The clergy will put forth almost superhuman efforts to shut away the light lest it should shine upon their flocks. By every means at their command they will endeavor to suppress the discussion of these vital questions. The church appeals to the strong arm of civil power, and, in this work, papists and Protestants unite. As the movement for Sunday enforcement becomes more bold and decided, the law will be invoked against commandment keepers. They will be threatened with fines and imprisonment, and some will be offered positions of influence, and other rewards and advantages, as inducements to renounce their faith. But their steadfast answer is: 'Show us from the Word of God our error-'the same

plea that was made by Luther under similar circumstances. Those who are arraigned before the courts make a strong vindication of the truth, and some who hear them are led to take their stand to keep all the commandments of God. Thus light will be brought before thousands who otherwise would know nothing of these truths. Conscientious obedience to the word of God will be treated as rebellion….as the defenders of truth refuse to honor the Sunday sabbath, some of them will be thrust into prison, some will be exiled, some will be treated as slaves. To human wisdom all this now seems impossible; but as the restraining Spirit of God shall be withdrawn from men, and they shall be under the control of Satan, who hates the divine precepts, there will be strange developments. The heart can be very cruel when Gods fear and love are removed. As the storm approaches, a large class who have professed faith in the third angels message, but have not been sanctified through obedience to the truth, abandon their position and join the ranks of the opposition. By uniting with the world and partaking of its spirit, they have come to view matters in nearly the same light; and when the test is brought, they are prepared to choose the easy, popular side. Men of talent and pleasing address, who once rejoiced in the truth, employ their powers to deceive and mislead souls. They become the most bitter enemies of their former brethren. When Sabbath-keepers are brought before the courts to answer for their faith, these apostates are the most efficient agents of Satan to misrepresent and accuse them and by false reports and insinuations to stir up the rulers against them." White, Great Controversy, 605-608

2. Revelation 18.

3. "Never will I leave you; never will I forsake you. So we say with confidence, The Lord is my helper; I will not be afraid. What can man do to me?" Hebrews 13:5, 6.

4. Matthew 10:36.

5. 'Do not forget to entertain strangers, for by so doing some people have entertained angels without knowing it.' Hebrews 13:2.

6. Isaiah 57:1, "The righteous perish and no one ponders it in his heart; devout men are taken away and no one understands that the righteous are taken away to be spared from evil."

Psalm 116:15, "Precious in the sight of the Lord is the death of His saints."

7. Matthew 10:36.

8. "Let him who does wrong continue to do wrong; let him who is vile continue to be vile, let him who does right continue to do right, and let him who is holy continue to be holy." Rev. 22: 11.

9. Rev. 20: 7-10.

10. Revelation 20: 7-10.

**Chapter 12**

1. The Bible teaches that salvation is a continuing experience. He that endures will be saved. ... Matt.24:13. Partakers of Christ if we hold fast... Heb. 3:6, 14.If any man will draw back... Heb.10:38... Lord prayed for Simons faith to fail not...Luke 22:32. Paul kept his body under subjection lest a castaway... 1 Cor. 9:27. Take heed lest ye fall... 1 Cor. 10:12, 13. Salvation nearer than when we believed... Rom. 13:11. These texts taken from The Bible Textionary.

2. "How repugnant to every emotion of love and mercy, and even to our sense of justice, is the doctrine that the wicked dead are tormented with fire and brimstone in an eternally burning hell; that for the sins of a brief earthly life they are to suffer torture as long as God shall live. Yet this doctrine has been widely taught and is still embodied in many of the creeds of Christendom. Said a learned doctor of divinity: "The sight of hell torments will exalt the happiness of the saints forever. When they see others who are of the same nature and born under the same circumstances, plunged in such misery, and they so distinguished, it will make them sensible of how happy they are." Another used these words: " While the decree of reprobation is eternally executing on the vessels of wrath, the smoke of their torment will be eternally ascending in view of the vessels of mercy, who, instead of taking the part of these miserable objects, will say, Amen, Alleluia! Praise ye the Lord!" Where in the pages of God's word, is such teaching to be found? Will the redeemed in heaven be lost to all emotions of pity and compassion, and even to feelings of common humanity? Are these to be exchanged for the indifference of the stoic or the cruelty of the savage? No! No! Such is not the teaching of the Book of God. Those who present the views expressed in the quotations given above may be learned and even honest men, but they are deluded by the sophistry of Satan. He leads them to misconstrue strong expressions of scripture, giving to the language the coloring of bitterness and malignity which pertains to himself, but not to our Creator.

'As I live, saith the Lord God, I have no pleasure in the death of the wicked; but that the wicked turn from his way and live: turn ye, turn ye from your evil ways; for why will ye die?' Ezekiel 33: 11. What would be gained to God should we admit that He delights in witnessing unceasing tortures; that He is regaled with the groans and shrieks and imprecations of the suffering creatures whom He holds in the flames of hell! Can these horrid sounds be music in the ear of Infinite Love? It is urged that the infliction of endless misery upon the wicked would show Gods hatred of sin as an evil which is ruinous to the peace and order of the universe. Oh, dreadful blasphemy! As if Gods hatred of sin is the reason why it is perpetuated. For, according to the teachings of these theologians, continued torture without hope of mercy maddens its wretched victims, and as they pour out their rage in curses and blasphemy, they are forever augmenting their load of guilt. God's glory is not enhanced by thus perpetuating continually increasing sin through ceaseless ages. It is beyond the power of the human mind to estimate the evil which has been wrought by the heresy of eternal torment. The religion of the Bible, full of love and goodness, and abounding in compassion, is darkened by superstition and clothed with terror. When we consider in what false colors Satan has painted the character of God, can we wonder that our merciful Creator is feared, dreaded and even hated? The appalling views of God which have spread over the world from the teachings of the pulpit have made thousands, yes, millions, of skeptics and infidels. The theory of eternal torment is one of the false doctrines that constitute the wine of the abomination of Babylon, of which she makes all nations drink. Revelation 14: 8; 17:2. That minister's of Christ should have accepted this heresy and proclaimed it from the sacred desk is indeed a mystery. They received it from Rome, as they received the false Sabbath. True, it has been taught by great and good men; but the light in this subject had not come to them as it has come to us. They were responsible only for the light which shone in their time; we are accountable for that which shines in our day. If we turn from the testimony of God's word, and accept false doctrines because our fathers taught them, we fall under the condemnation pronounced upon Babylon; we are drinking of the wine of her abominations." White, Great Controversy, 535-537. Also see Revelation 22:11.

3. "As the opposition rises to a fiercer height, the servants of God are again perplexed; for it seems to them that they have brought the crisis. But conscience and the word of God assure them that their course is right; and although the trials continue, they are strengthened to bear them. The contest grows closer and sharper, but their faith and courage rise with the emergency." "Christ's ambassadors have nothing to do with consequences. They must perform their duty and leave results with God." Ibid, 609, 610

4. "As the defenders of truth refuse to honor the Sunday-sabbath, some of them will be thrust into prison." Ibid, 608

5. Seventh-day Adventist Hymnal, Review and Herald Pub. Assoc., 1987) 321.

## Chapter 13

1. Often manipulative tactics such as lies are used with prisoners that involve

### Chapter 15
1. Psalm 91; Heb. 13;5, 6.
2. Matthew 6: 26.
3. See Appendix Ch. 11: 3.
4. John 8: 32.
5. Acts 17: 11.
6. "Of course the Catholic church claims that the change [Sabbath to Sunday] was her act. And the act is a mark of her ecclesiastical power and authority in religious matters." C.F. Thomas, Chancellor of Cardinal Gibbons

"I have repeatedly offered $1,000 to anyone who can prove to me from the Bible alone that I am bound to keep Sunday holy. There is no such law in the Bible. It is a law of the holy Catholic Church alone. The Bible says, remember that thou keep holy the Sabbath day. The Catholic Church says, No! by my divine power I abolish the Sabbath day, and command you to keep holy the first day of the week. And, Lo, The entire civilized world bows down in reverent obedience to the command of the holy Catholic Church." Father Enright, President of Redemptorist College

"Have you any other way of proving that the Church has power to institute festivals of precept?

Had she not such power, she could not have done that in which all modern religionists agree with her; she could not have substituted the observance of Sunday the first day of the week, for the observance of Saturday the Seventh day, a change for which there is no scriptural authority." A Doctrinal Catechism, 174.

"Sunday is a Catholic institution, and its claims to observance can be defended only on Catholic principles... From beginning to end of scripture there is not a single passage that warrants the transfer of weekly public worship from the last day of the week to the first." Catholic Press (Sydney, Australia, August 1900)

Reason and common sense demand the acceptance of one or the other of these alternatives: either Protestantism and the keeping holy of Saturday, or Catholicity and the keeping holy of Sunday. Compromise is impossible." The Catholic Mirror (Dec. 23, 1893)

Where did Sunday observance come from?

"In ancient Babylonia the sun was worshipped from immemorial antiquity." THE WORSHIP OF NATURE, Vol. 1, p. 529

"On the venerable day of the Sun let the Magistrates and people residing in the cities rest and let all workshops be closed." Edict of Constantine, A.D. 321

"Paganism must still have been an operative belief with the man... He was at best half heathen, half Christian. Who could seek to combine the worship of Christ with the worship of Apollo (child of the sun-god), having the name of one and figure of the other impressed upon his coins." ENCYCLOPEDIA BRITANNICA: Article 'Constantine'

"The sun was a foremost god with heathendom... Hence the church [Catholic Church] would seem to have said, 'keep that old pagan name. it shall remain consecrated, sanctified,' and thus the pagan Sunday, dedicated to Balder [sun-god], became the Christian Sunday, sacred to Jesus." THE CATHOLIC WORLD, (March, 1894), 809

"The church has always had a strong sense of its own authority... Perhaps the boldest thing, the most revolutionary change the Church ever did, happened in the first century. The holy day, the Sabbath, was changed from Saturday to Sunday. 'The day of the Lord' (dies Dominica) was chosen, not from any directions noted in the

Scriptures, but from the Church's sense of its own power... People who think that the Scriptures should be the sole authority, should logically become 7$^{th}$ Day Adventists, and keep Saturday holy." Sentinel, St Catherine Catholic Church, Algonac, MI (May 21, 1995)

What Do Protestants Say About Sunday?

Episcopalian: "The observance of the first day instead of the seventh day rests on the testimony of the Catholic church, and the [Catholic] church alone." Hobart Church News, July 2, 1894

Baptist: "There was and is a commandment to keep holy the Sabbath day, but that Sabbath day was not Sunday. It will be said, however, and with some show of triumph, that the Sabbath was transferred from the seventh to the first day of the week... Where can the record of such a transaction be found? Not in the New Testament- absolutely not.... Of course, I quite well know that Sunday did come to use in early Christian history as a religious day, as we learn from the Christian Fathers, and other sources. But what a pity that it comes branded with the mark of paganism, and christened with the name of the sun-god, when adopted and sanctioned by the papal apostasy, and bequeathed as a sacred legacy to Protestantism!" Dr. Edward T. Hiscox (author of the Baptist Manual)

Lutheran: "They [the Catholics] allege the Sabbath changed into Sunday, the Lords Day, contrary to the Decalogue, as it appears, neither is there any example more boasted of than the changing of the Sabbath day. Great, say they, is the power and authority of the Church [Church of Rome], since it dispensed with one of the Ten Commandments." Martin Luther, Augsburg Confession of Faith, Art.28, Par. 9.

Dwight L. Moody: "The Sabbath was binding in Eden, and it has been in force ever since. This fourth commandment begins with the word 'remember', showing that the Sabbath already existed when God wrote the law on the tables of stone at Sinai. How can men claim that this one commandment has been done away with when they will admit that the other nine are still binding?" D.L. Moody, Weighted and Wanting, p.47.

Presbyterian: "The Sabbath is a part of the Decalogue- the Ten Commandments. This alone forever settles the question as to the perpetuity of the institution... Until, therefore, it can be shown that the whole moral law has been repealed, the Sabbath will stand.... The teaching of Christ confirms the perpetuity of the Sabbath." T.C. Blake, D.D., Theology Condensed, pp. 474,475.

Methodist: "It is true that there is no positive command for infant baptism. Nor is there any for keeping holy the first day of the week. Many believe that Christ changed the Sabbath. But, from His own words, we see that He came for no such purpose. Those that believe that Jesus changed the Sabbath base it only on supposition." Amos Binney, Theological Compendium, pp. 180,181 [He authored a Methodist New Testament Commentary, and his Methodist "Compendium" was published for forty years.]

7. It was the experience of the author to go through much confusion on this and some other winds of doctrine unfounded in scripture. Through much study though he has come to realize that the most important message for these last hours of earth's history is to spread the message of Revelation 14. In the end, it will be seen that character will be what determines our eternal destiny.

8. The study on tongues is a very controversial subject in some circles. With all feelings and experiences aside one will discover as did the author of this book that depending solely on the scriptural study of this topic will help one realize that tongues speaking was and always has been for the promoting of the Gospel as can be seen in the scriptural references below. Acts 2:1-11; 1 Corinthians 12, 13 and 14. Nowhere in these scriptures are tongues used for the edification of self but were given for spreading the Gospel quickly to the world which would have otherwise been impossible because of the language barriers. See also Rene Noorbergens book Charisma of the Spirit. This book searches out the background of the modern tongues movement and is very enlightening for the avid reader. To the question as to whether or not as Christians we should pray for the gift of tongues it would be wiser to pray for the Holy Spirit to guide us into all truth (John 16:13), rather than to pray for the gift of tongues. Our great adversary, the devil, is using the gift of tongues in the most subtle manner today, to ensnare and capture souls. "And I saw three unclean spirits like frogs come out of the mouth of the dragon, and out of the mouth of the beast, and out of the mouth of the false prophet. For they are the spirits of devils, working miracles." Revelation 16: 13, 14. (KJV) These spirits of devils are "like frogs". How do frogs catch their prey? With their tongues! And in the last days,

these spirits of devils "like frogs" are using a counterfeit gift of tongues to ensnare multitudes of Christians unawares. If a person doesn't know what they are saying when speaking in an unknown tongues (the supposed gift of tongues) how do they know that they are not blaspheming God? At the tower of Babel we see how God confused the languages (Genesis 11). Babylon literally means "confusion". Confusion of tongues is a primary characteristic of ancient Babylon, and the book of Revelation reveals that there is a modern, spiritual Babylon! When we look at the Bible we see that the genuine gift of tongues were actual languages, known somewhere in the world. "And they were all filled with the Holy Ghost, and began to speak with other tongues as the Spirit gave them utterance. And there were dwelling at Jerusalem Jews, devout men, out of every nation under heaven. Now when this was noised abroad, the multitude came together, and were confounded, because that every man heard them speak in his *own language.* (italics supplied) And they were all amazed and marveled, saying one to another, Behold, are not all these which speak Galileans? And how hear we every man in his own tongue, wherein we were born? Parthians, and Medes, and Elamites, and the dwellers in Mesopotamia, and in Judea, and Cappadocia, in Pontus, and Asia, Phrygia, and Pamphylia, in Egypt, and in the parts of Libya about Cyrene, and strangers of Rome, Jews and proselytes, Cretes and Arabians, we do hear them speak in our tongues the wonderful works of God." Acts 2:4-11) (KJV) .One might ask why the gift of tongues was given in the New Testament church to the new converts? The New Testament Church needed the gift of tongues because how else, without knowing all the languages of the earth, could these uneducated laymen have been able to carry the Gospel to the entire world without it. (See Matthew 28:19).

9. This study is taken from The Bible Textionary. Quotes from the KJV Bible. This booklet deals with many Bible topics and can be purchased from the Adventist Book Center. 'Thy way O God, is in the sanctuary'. Psalm 77:13. "The earthly Tabernacle Patterned After Heavenly Tabernacle" Let them make me a sanctuary; that I may dwell among them. Made after heavenly pattern Hebrews 8:5; Exodus 15:17; 25:8, 9; Tabernacle on earth blessed by cloud of the Lord by day and fire by night. Exodus 40:38; Sanctuary on earth faced East so worshippers turned back on Sun opposite to Sun worshippers. Exodus 26:18, 20, 22:

Ezekiel 8:16; Original- Lord pitched, not man. Hebrews 8:1, 2, 5; 9:11: Temple of the Tabernacle of the testimony in heaven opened. Revelation 15:5. 'Two Apartments in Tabernacles' Two apartments –after second veil. Hebrews 9:1-3; Earthly first apartment furnishings also seen in heaven-7 lamps, golden altar. Revelation 4:1-5; 8:3; Earthly second apartment contents also seen in heaven- the ark. Revelation 11:19. 'Ark of Testimony in Tabernacles- God's Throne' Ark of Gods testimony. Exodus 25:16,21;31:18; Mercy Seat above Ark, Gods earthly throne- will commune with thee. Exodus 25; 22; Ark and Mercy Seat in Most Holy Place. Exodus 26: 34; Ark of His Testament in Temple of God. Revelation 11: 19; Heavenly Throne. Revelation 4: 1-11 Gods Throne in Heaven- A most Holy place because of His presence. Revelation 4:2 'Priests, High Priest in Earthly- High Priest in Heavenly' Aaron and some anointed for priests office of earthly tabernacle. Exodus 40: 12-15; Leviticus 1: 5-9 Priests serve unto example and shadow of heavenly things. Hebrews 8:5 Christ is High Priest minister of sanctuary, true tabernacle, Lord pitched, not man. Hebrews 8:1,2 All things made according to pattern shewed in mount. Hebrews 8:5 Our great high priest. Heb.3: 1; 4:14 He ever liveth to make intercession. Heb. 7:25 'Earthly High Priest Imperfect- Heavenly High Priest Perfect' Earthly high priest had sins, infirmities. Heb. 7: 27,28; Lev. 4: 3-12 Earthly high priest human. Heb. 5:1 Heavenly high priest undefiled, consecrated for evermore. Heb. 7: 26-28 Jesus our high priest passed into the heavens. Heb. 4: 14,15 Heavenly high priest on the right hand of throne of majesty in heaven. Heb. 4: 14; 8:1 He ever liveth to make intercession for them. Christ our advocate. Heb. 7: 25; 1 John 2:1 'Sacrifices Offered For Sins' Earthly high priests offered daily sacrifice for self and people. Heb. 7:27 Animal sacrifices as sin offerings- Levitical laws. Lev. 1 through 11 Blood necessary for atonement. Lev. 4: 27- 35; 17:11,14 High Priest higher than heavens offered sacrifice once when He offered Himself. Heb. 7:27 Christ " the more perfect tabernacle" to minister "His own blood". Heb. 9: 11-14 'Cleansing of Tabernacles' He (earthly priest) shall make atonement for the holy place annually. Lev. 16: 16,29-34; Heb. 9: 7,25 Christ is not entered into holy place made by man but into heaven itself... once in end of world after this the judgment. Heb. 9: 23-28 Unto two thousand and three hundred days; then shall the sanctuary be cleansed. Daniel 8: 13,14; Heb. 9:23. ' 2300 Day Prophecy Began

457 BC So Ends 1844 AD Based On Day For Year Principle' Decree to rebuild Jerusalem, 457 BC, beginning of seventy weeks, first part of 2300 day prophecy. Daniel 9:25; Ezra 4:7-23; 7: 1-26 Unto two thousand and three hundred days; then shall the sanctuary be cleansed. Daniel 8: 13,14; Heb. 9:23. Day for year principle. Numbers 14:34; Ezekiel 4:6. Daniel has vision concluded with 2300 day prophecy. Dan.8:1-14. Gabriel explains vision to Daniel. Dan. 8: 15-26. Daniel fainted and was sick from astonishment of vision before understanding vision. Dan. 8:27. Daniel studies prophecies of Jeremiah and prays for understanding. Dan. 9:21-23. Gabriel explains the vision further with another time period of seventy weeks, beginning at commandment to restore and rebuild Jerusalem. (457 BC) Daniel 9: 24-27. 'Earthly Tabernacle Service Ended At Jesus Death- Heavenly Tabernacle In Existence To End' Sacrifice and oblation to cease at Jesus death. Dan. 9:26, 27. Earthly tabernacle service ended at Jesus death. Veil of the temple rent from top to bottom. Matthew 27:50, 51; Mark 15:37, 38; Luke 23:45, 46. Tabernacle of testimony opened in heaven after Christ's atoning sacrifice and ascension. Heb. 8: 1-3; 9:8-14; Acts 5:31. Temple of God opened in heaven, ark of His testament seen. Rev. 11:18, 19. 'Gods Dwelling Place New Earth' Behold the tabernacle of God is with men, and He will dwell with them. Rev.21:1–3.

**Chapter 16**
1. Rev. 2: 10.
2. Rev. 6.
3. Rev. 6: 15,16.
4. Isaiah 25: 9.
5. Matthew 24:30; 26:64: 1 Thess. 4:14-17; Rev. 1:7

**Chapter 17**
1. Rev.13:15.
2. 1 Thess. 4: 13-17.
3. Luke 23:34.

We invite you to view the complete
selection of titles we publish at:

www.AspectBooks.com

Scan with your mobile
device to go directly
to our website.

Please write or email us your praises, reactions, or
thoughts about this or any other book we publish at:

# ASPECT Books
## www.ASPECTBooks.com

P.O. Box 954
Ringgold, GA 30736

info@AspectBooks.com

Aspect Books titles may be purchased in bulk for
educational, business, fund-raising, or sales promotional use.
For information, please e-mail:

BulkSales@AspectBooks.com

Finally, if you are interested in seeing
your own book in print, please contact us at:

publishing@AspectBooks.com

We would be happy to review your manuscript for free.

CPSIA information can be obtained at www.ICGtesting.com
Printed in the USA
LVOW130055021012
301060LV00007B/20/P